Trends
in Outside Support
for Insurgent
Movements

Daniel Byman

Peter Chalk

Bruce Hoffman

William Rosenau

David Brannan

Prepared for the Office of Transnational Issues

National Security Research Division

RAND

The research described in this report was sponsored by the Office of Transnational Issues. The research was conducted through the International Security and Defense Policy Center (ISDPC) of RAND's National Security Research Division (NSRD).

Library of Congress Cataloging-in-Publication Data

Trends in outside support for insurgent movements / Daniel Byman ... [et al.].
    p. cm.
    "MR-1405."
    Includes bibliographical references.
    ISBN 0-8330-3052-3
    1. Insurgency. 2. World politics—1989– I. Byman, Daniel, 1967–

    JC328.5 .T74 2001
    322.4'2—dc21

                                    2001048219

RAND is a nonprofit institution that helps improve policy and decisionmaking through research and analysis. RAND® is a registered trademark. RAND's publications do not necessarily reflect the opinions or policies of its research sponsors.

Cover design by Maritta Tapanainen

Published 2001 by RAND
1700 Main Street, P.O. Box 2138, Santa Monica, CA 90407-2138
1200 South Hayes Street, Arlington, VA 22202-5050
201 North Craig Street, Suite 102, Pittsburgh, PA 15213
RAND URL: http://www.rand.org/
To order RAND documents or to obtain additional information,
contact Distribution Services: Telephone: (310) 451-7002;
Fax: (310) 451-6915; Email: order@rand.org

This report assesses post–Cold War trends in external support for insurgent movements. It describes the frequency with which states, diasporas, refugees, and other non-state actors back guerrilla movements. It also assesses the motivations of these actors and which types of support matter most. The report concludes by assessing the implications for analysts of insurgent movements.

This report's findings should be of particular interest to the intelligence community, policy analysts, and scholars who seek to better understand the nature of insurgency in a post–Cold War era. This study should also be of interest to U.S. government policymakers concerned with adapting American foreign and defense policy to address the challenges posed by insurgent movements today and in the future.

This research was conducted within the International Security and Defense Policy Center (ISDPC) of RAND's National Security Research Division (NSRD). NSRD conducts research and analysis for a broad range of clients, including the U.S. Department of Defense, allied foreign governments, the intelligence community and foundations.

CONTENTS

FIGURE

TABLES

State support or sponsorship of an insurgency as an instrument of foreign policy was common during the Cold War. The United States, the Soviet Union, and a host of regional powers backed their favored proxies, often transforming local quarrels into international contests. The end of the Cold War did not end the use of insurgents, but the dimensions and nature of outside aid and the identity of the providers have changed significantly. Hundreds of millions of dollars no longer regularly flow from Washington's and Moscow's coffers. Leading state sponsors today such as Iran, Rwanda, Angola, and Pakistan, for example, devote far smaller amounts of money and resources to their proxies. Indeed, state support is no longer the only, or necessarily the most important, game in town. Diasporas have played a particularly important role in sustaining several strong insurgencies. More rarely, refugees, guerrilla groups, or other types of non-state supporters play a significant role in creating or sustaining an insurgency, offering fighters, training, or other important forms of support.

This report analyzes these changes in the nature of outside support for insurgencies starting with the end of the Cold War.[1] It describes the nature and motivations of state backers and examines the role of diasporas, refugees, and other non-state supporters of insurgencies. The report concludes by assessing which forms of outside support

---

[1] A complete accounting, of course, would require a survey of Cold War insurgencies as well as those in the post–Cold War period, something we do not attempt in this report. However, we instead draw on secondary literature from the Cold War period to make many of our conclusions regarding comparisons of the two periods.

are most important and also offers implications for the analysis of insurgency today.

STATE SUPPORT FOR INSURGENCIES

State support has had a profound impact on the effectiveness of many rebel movements since the end of the Cold War. In Asia, Africa, Europe, and the Middle East, states have supported many insurgencies. Out of the 74 post–Cold War insurgencies surveyed, state support, we believe, played a major role in initiating, sustaining, bringing to victory, or otherwise assisting 44 of them. In contrast to the Cold War period, however, neighboring states constitute the vast majority of state supporters.

States supporting insurgents are primarily motivated by geopolitics rather than ideology, ethnic affinity, or religious sentiment. Although these less-strategic rationales at times played an important role in states' decisions to support insurgencies, they are far less frequent motivations compared to increasing regional influence, destabilizing neighborhood rivals, or otherwise ensuring that a regime has a loud voice in local affairs. Indeed, when ethnic kin or religious brethren do receive support, it is usually done to further realpolitik ambitions.

States can offer insurgents a wide range of assistance. They often provide fighters with arms, money, and materiel. In addition, states can offer insurgents a safe place to organize and train as well as offer various types of diplomatic assistance, including helping them represent their cause in international fora and with major powers. Sometimes state support is more ineffable: The encouragement or example of the state is enough to convince individuals to take up arms and join, or otherwise support, an insurgent movement.

DIASPORAS: AN EMERGING PLAYER?

Diasporas—immigrant communities established in foreign countries—frequently support insurgencies in their homelands. Diasporas have played an important role in helping Tamil rebels in Sri Lanka, Kurdish guerrillas in Turkey, and the Palestine Liberation Organization (PLO), among other movements. Diasporas may become more important to insurgencies in the future because, unlike states, they are more reliable in funding and do not seek to exert control over a movement. In addition, ethnic insurgencies, which are growing in number relative to ideological ones, have an already-established bond with immigrant communities that they can exploit.

In contrast to states, diasporas are largely motivated by ethnic affinity. Indeed, almost inherent to the idea of a diaspora is the concept of homeland. Communities abroad often feel a genuine sympathy for the struggles of their brethren elsewhere. At times, they may also feel a sense of guilt that they are safe while those left behind are enmeshed in brutal and bloody conflict. Insurgent groups actively play on this sympathy and guilt to secure critical financial and political support. When such support is not forthcoming, insurgents sometimes resort to coercion.

Diaspora support can play a critical role in financially sustaining a movement, but does not offer the same spectrum of benefits that states can provide. Financial assistance is far and away the most common form of assistance that diasporas provide to insurgent movements. Certain migrant communities also provide a range of other aid—although this occurs less frequently. Armenian, Kurdish, and Tamil diasporas have, for instance, generated political pressure on their various host governments to help insurgents or to otherwise oppose the governments they are fighting. Members of the Tamil diaspora have acted as de facto political representatives of the Tamil Tigers while skilled individuals, such as computer programmers, have assisted with the group's military and fundraising efforts. Hezbollah has also used the Lebanese Shi'a diaspora to gather intelligence abroad, including information that has aided the group in conducting terrorist attacks on Israeli targets overseas.

Shutting down diaspora support requires action by states hosting large numbers of immigrants who back insurgencies. Several problems, however, hinder these efforts. Host governments often have difficulty differentiating between non-insurgent immigrants and activists. Moreover, the insurgency may exercise tremendous political clout through its diaspora. At times, governments may not be able to exercise sufficient control to shut down a diaspora's activities.

The strength and longevity of diaspora support also depends heavily on the nature of the countries that host the immigrants. Two particularly important policies to monitor are (1) the host government's willingness to actively police immigrant communities and (2) the host society's own willingness to assimilate immigrants. If insurgents can be prevented from controlling migrant communities, involuntary support is likely to decrease. Moreover, if diasporas are allowed to assimilate into their adopted countries, links with their homeland and associated identification with the objectives of insurgents operating there often diminish.

OTHER NON-STATE SUPPORT

Refugees, foreign guerrilla movements, religious organizations, wealthy individuals, and even human rights groups have all played important roles in fostering and sustaining insurgent movements. Of this disparate group of additional supporters, refugees are usually the most significant. Refugee flows and insurgencies often feed each other: The discrimination, violence, and misery that typically accompany civil wars often produce refugees who in turn contribute to the original conflict. Poor and lacking even basic resources, displaced populations can seldom offer arms or money. Refugees do provide manpower for an insurgent organization, particularly in the aftermath of mass population upheaval and displacement.

Indeed, refugees have played an important role in many insurgencies. The Taliban was formed among displaced Afghans, particularly those who became seminary students in Pakistan. Karen refugees helped sustain the Karen National Union's resistance to the Burmese government, while Palestinian refugees helped sustain the PLO for decades before the Oslo Agreement. Hutus and Tutsis who fled from Rwanda and Burundi played a critical role in supporting conflict in these countries and, after the war spread to the Congo, refugees from the fighting there also often joined insurgent movements.[2]

Refugees generally are motivated by a powerful desire to regain their homeland or to restore their nation's influence over part of a territory. Refugees may also back insurgents for protection from preda-

---

[2]For a review, see Uvin (1999), pp. 253–272.

tory governments in their host country, rival groups, or bandit forces. When rebel movements control refugee camps, coercion can often explain why refugees proffer their support. As with diasporas, support of the nation hosting the refugees is often critical when refugees seek to assist insurgents in their home countries. Strong states can use refugees as their pawns or proxies or, if the government prefers, prevent them from aiding insurgents. If the state is too weak to impose its will, displaced communities can often act with impunity.

In addition to refugees, other non-state supporters have sometimes increased an insurgency's military power, financial position, or diplomatic influence. Charles Taylor's guerrilla organization, for example, sponsored the Revolutionary United Front in Sierra Leone and used it to destabilize the entire country. Religious organizations, particularly Islamic ones, have channeled money, arms, and volunteers to several religiously oriented insurgencies. Relief agencies have often inadvertently provided food, havens, or publicity for guerrilla groups. Wealthy individuals have also at times made generous contributions that have helped insurgents sustain their effort. Overall, these other non-state supporters generally have not had the same impact on insurgencies as states, diasporas, and refugees.

ASSESSING OUTSIDE SUPPORT

The value of outside support depends on the requirements of the insurgency, its ability to acquire what it needs domestically, the strength of the state, and other factors that vary with each movement. In general, several forms of outside support have proven particularly important:

- Safe havens are essential to the success of any guerrilla movement, providing insurgents with sanctuary from government attacks and a place in which to arm, train, organize, and stage operations as well as to rest and recuperate.

- Money also has a powerful effect on insurgent movements. Funds can be used to buy weapons, bribe local officials, pay operatives to write propaganda, provide a social network that builds a popular base, and otherwise serve a myriad of purposes. Because conflict areas are often cash-poor, even a little financial support often goes a long way.

- States may also provide political support, giving insurgents access to their diplomatic apparatus, pushing for recognition of the insurgent movement in international fora, encouraging aid agencies to provide assistance to the group directly, and otherwise championing the insurgent cause. In addition, political support often involves denying assistance to the government the insurgents oppose.

- States at times provide direct military support, using their own armies to fight alongside insurgents. Direct support is rare, but when it occurs it often greatly facilitates insurgent efforts to defeat opposing government forces.

Other forms of support, while often helpful and sometimes vital, are generally less useful to insurgents. Training is valuable, particularly in the early days of an insurgency, but most successful movements learn to train themselves over time. Weapons are always desirable, but insurgents can often buy or steal what they need. Refugees and diasporas often directly aid insurgents by providing fighters, although outside volunteers seldom add appreciable numbers to the overall insurgent cause. In addition, outsiders may provide intelligence, but successful insurgencies almost invariably are skilled at collecting their own information. Finally, outsiders may help insurgents organize or inspire them to fight. Again, this assistance is most valuable in the early stages of an insurgency but appears less significant over time and even peripheral to well-established movements.

Assistance from external sponsors produces costs as well as benefits for insurgents. Foreign manpower, while helping to fill depleted guerrilla ranks, can lead to a loss of nationalist credibility and, if human rights abuses occur, an erosion of local and international support. A large influx of money to insurgents can contribute to corruption, attendant criminality, feuding, and internal discord. More broadly, external aid can decrease an insurgent movement's freedom of action. Outside patrons, particularly states, typically seek some measure of control in exchange for their investments. State support is often fickle, and insurgents who depend on it too much risk disaster.

When judging the impact of outside support, understanding timing is essential. Because the logistical requirements to create an insurgency are minimal or modest at best, other guerrilla movements, religious organizations, or poor or weak states can by themselves facilitate the emergence of a movement—although ensuring its success is considerably more difficult. Insurgencies that seek more than survival in the face of a government counterinsurgency campaign, however, must make a qualitative leap in their organizational, political, and military efforts. Outsiders can help groups through this transition, but most of the burden inevitably falls on insurgents themselves.

At times, outside actors' passivity has more of an impact than any formal support they provide. Diasporas and other interested outsiders often openly raise money, distribute propaganda, and otherwise aid an insurgency's cause with little interference from a host government even when that government may generally oppose the insurgent movement and favor the government the insurgent is fighting. Similarly, refugees are at times allowed to organize and freely support an insurgent movement with little interference.

The end of the Cold War has fundamentally changed the role that external actors play in insurgent conflicts. Understanding insurgent struggles today requires recognizing the changing agendas and limited means of state sponsors, the possible increase in the role of diasporas, and the rise of other non-state backers. These outside actors are not all equally important, and their impact varies according to the needs of the insurgent movement and the context of its struggle. However, recognizing the new roles and limits of outside backers is essential for understanding the dynamics of insurgency today.

ACKNOWLEDGMENTS

This report benefited from the insights and assistance of many people. The authors interviewed many analysts at the Central Intelligence Agency (CIA) who were generous with their expertise on various insurgencies and on the problem of outside support for insurgency in general. Several other CIA officials provided vital administrative support and proved valuable critics of earlier versions of this report. These individuals have asked not to be acknowledged by name, but we thank them all.

Brian Jenkins of RAND and Benjamin Valentino of Harvard's Center for Security and International Affairs reviewed this document. Both offered useful reviews that strengthened our analysis and sharpened our conclusions. Olga Oliker and Bruce Pirnie shared their knowledge of conflicts in the former Soviet Union and the Balkans, respectively. Risha Henneman and Chi San assisted in gathering and assembling data as well as preparing the final document. Stuart Johnson and Kevin O'Connell helped steer the project and ensure that all the wheels turned smoothly.

ADF	Allied Democratic Forces
ANC	African National Congress
AUC	Autodefensas Unidas de Colombia
CID	Criminal Investigation Department
CIS	Commonwealth of Independent States
CRD	Congolese Rally for Democracy
CRD-ML	CRD–Liberation Movement
ECOMOG	Economic Community of West African States Monitoring Group
FACT	Federation of Associations of Canadian Tamils
FARC	Revolutionary Armed Forces of Colombia
FTO	Foreign terrorist organization
IMU	Islamic Movement of Uzbekistan
IPKF	Indian Peacekeeping Force
ISI	Inter-Services Intelligence
JKLF	Jammu and Kashmir Liberation Front
JUI	Jamiat-ul-Ulema-e-Islam
KLA	Kosovo Liberation Army
LRA	Lord's Resistance Army

LTTE	Liberation Tigers of Tamil Eelam
MEK	Mujahedin-e Khalq
MLC	Movement for the Liberation of the Congo
NA	Northern Alliance
NGO	Nongovernmental organization
NPFL	National Patriotic Front of Liberia
PAC	Pan-African Congress
PIRA	Provisional Irish Republican Army
PKK	Kurdish Workers Party
PLO	Palestine Liberation Organization
RUF	Revolutionary United Front
SAIRI	Supreme Assembly for the Islamic Revolution in Iraq
SLAF	Sri Lankan Armed Forces
ULIMO	United Liberation Movement for Democracy
UN	United Nations
UNITA	National Union for the Total Independence of Angola
UTO	United Tamil Organization
WTM	World Tamil Movement

Chapter One

INTRODUCTION

State support or sponsorship of an insurgency as an instrument of foreign policy was common during the Cold War. The United States used the Nicaraguan contras, the Afghan mujahedin, Tibetan Buddhist fighters, and other insurgent movements as part of its policy to contain (and occasionally roll back) communism. Washington was not alone: The Soviet Union and China backed communist guerrillas in Angola, Greece, South Africa, Vietnam, and other parts of the world to further their influence.[1] Regional powers also recognized the utility of insurgencies. Countries as diverse as Israel, Iran, South Africa, Pakistan, Sudan, and Ethiopia were among those that supported insurgencies to promote their local interests.

The end of the Cold War, however, did not end state support for insurgents. Russia supported clients in several former republics of the Soviet Union, enabling them to gain autonomy and sometimes take power. In Africa, Rwanda and Uganda both assisted rebels who overthrew the Mobutu regime in Zaire. Currently, almost all of the Congo's neighbors actively assist one faction or another enmeshed in the country's civil war. Although the United States no longer arms anticommunist insurgents, it has provided aid to anti-Baath groups in Iraq and has at times considered providing direct assistance to groups as diverse as Bosnian Muslims, the Kosovo Liberation Army (KLA), Iranian opposition movements, and Christian and animist Sudanese fighters.

---

[1] For an overview of U.S. and Soviet support for insurgent movements, see Shafer (1988); Blaufarb (1977); Tanham and Duncanson (1970), pp. 113–122; Odom (1992); Eckstein (1964); and Leites and Wolf (1970).

Of the 74 insurgencies active since 1991 that were surveyed for this report, 44 received state support that, in our judgment, was significant or critical to the survival and success of the movement (several other insurgencies received state support that was of limited consequence). Other outside supporters were also active: 21 movements received significant support from refugees, 19 received significant support from diasporas, and 25 gained backing from other outside actors, such as Islamic organizations or relief agencies. A complete listing of outside support for the post-1991 insurgencies we surveyed is given in Appendix A.

State support, accordingly, remains an important source of strength for many insurgencies in the post–Cold War world. Outside government assistance helps insurgents improve their military power, recruiting base, diplomatic leverage, and other ingredients to success. Reflecting this, many of the insurgencies that have achieved the most impressive objectives, or remained operationally effective for extended periods of time—for example, the African National Congress (ANC), the Lebanese Hezbollah, the forces of Laurent Kabila in Zaire (now the Democratic Republic of the Congo), the pro–Commonwealth of Independent States (CIS) Tajiks, the Abkhaz, Transnistrians, the Palestine Liberation Organization (PLO), the Nicaraguan resistance, and the Taliban—have all received a large measure of state assistance. In several instances, the insurgents won and gained control of government and the country with the direct assistance of their backers' military forces.

While outside support for insurgencies has continued since the end of the Cold War, the dimensions and nature of this aid and the identity of the providers have changed significantly. Although both the United States and Russia, to varying degrees, still offer insurgents support, hundreds of millions of dollars no longer regularly flow from Washington's and Moscow's coffers. Iran and Pakistan are two of the most significant post–Cold War backers of insurgencies, but the resources they devote for this purpose pale in comparison to the support once offered by the United States and the Soviet Union.

Indeed, state support is no longer the only, or necessarily the most important, game in town. Diasporas have played a particularly important role in sustaining several strong insurgencies. The Palestinian, Irish, Tamil, and Kurdish diasporas, for example, have helped foster strong insurgencies that have weathered concerted attacks of dedicated states. Diasporas play a particularly important role in funding and, although precise figures are unavailable, have probably surpassed states as the main financial sources for insurgencies today. Diaspora support has tended to be far more reliable than state support, which is more likely to suddenly disappear or be reduced.

Support has also come from other types of non-state actors, including refugees, guerrilla groups, and individuals. Some of these non-state actors have played a significant role in creating or sustaining an insurgency, offering fighters, training militants, giving money, or providing other important forms of support. Afghan refugees swelled the ranks of the Taliban, enabling the movement to conquer much of Afghanistan. Insurgent groups such as Hezbollah or Liberia's National Patriotic Front have armed and trained guerrilla fighters in third countries, helping to launch often-potent cross-border rebel movements. Religious organizations such as Usama bin Laden's Al Qaeda network and even wealthy individuals have at times also made substantial contributions to insurgent movements. Understanding the nature of external backing today requires recognizing the important contributions of this widening range of non-state actors.

Both state and non-state support for an insurgency can make a movement far more effective, prolong the war, increase the scale and lethality of its struggle, and may even transform a civil conflict into an international war. Like other foreign policy tools, the effects can be both positive and negative; they are also often unpredictable. Although the actual overthrow of an enemy government is relatively rare (though not unheard of), the aid provided to an insurgency can often produce a number of less-ambitious benefits, such as weakening a hostile government and strengthening a rival group's bid for power or simply demonstrating support for ethnic kin. At the same time, external support can provoke other parties to intervene, escalating limited strife into full-blown conflict. Such diffusion and escalation is often difficult to anticipate and can produce greater instability. Insurgent movements themselves often face a difficult dilemma: Although they have much to gain from outside support, it often comes with a price, imposing undesirable political or military restrictions and even diminishing a group's legitimacy.

In recent years, however, the issue of external support for insurgencies has received relatively scant attention, given the end of the Cold War and the demise of a U.S.-Soviet rivalry. This report attempts to fill some of the conceptual and intellectual gaps by surveying the current status of outside support for insurgent movements and assessing its impact and implications. Specifically, it seeks to answer the following four key questions:

- What are the external sources of support for insurgencies today?

- What are the characteristics and motivations of the supporters?

- What key differences can be discerned between state and non-state supporters?

- On what aspects of an insurgency's struggle does outside support have the most and least impact?

The purpose of this research is to help intelligence analysts better identify the factors that affect the conduct of insurgencies and better predict their success or failure. Focusing specifically on outside support for insurgencies may prove particularly promising, as it offers a means through which policymakers can influence an insurgency's progress without direct intervention in the country in question.

WHAT IS AN INSURGENCY?

This study uses the definition of insurgencies provided in the pamphlet *Guide to the Analysis of Insurgency*, published by the Central Intelligence Agency (n.d., p. 2) in the 1980s. This definition states:

> Insurgency is a protracted political-military activity directed toward completely or partially controlling the resources of a country through the use of irregular military forces and illegal political organizations. Insurgent activity—including guerrilla warfare, terrorism, and political mobilization, for example, propaganda, recruitment, front and covert party organization, and international activity—is designed to weaken government control and legitimacy while increasing insurgent control and legitimacy. The common denominator of most insurgent groups is their desire to control a particular area. This objective differentiates insurgent groups from purely terrorist organizations, whose objectives do not include the

creation of an alternative government capable of controlling a given area or country.

Several aspects of this definition are particularly important to note. First, insurgents engage in a range of activities, most notably guerrilla warfare, but also political mobilization and attendant efforts to attract support from abroad. Thus, measures of the effectiveness of outside support must look beyond the immediate physical impact on the battlefield and take into account the political as well as military dimensions of the insurgent's overall struggle. Second, terrorism in this context is a specific tactic that insurgents use as part of a broader strategy to control a particular geographic area.[2] That is, terrorism is an auxiliary mode of violence rather than an exclusive one. While both the Liberation Tigers of Tamil Eelam (LTTE), a group fighting in Sri Lanka, and Lebanon's Hezbollah may be among the world's bloodiest practitioners of terrorism, they are also considered insurgent movements for the purposes of this report because they use a range of other tactics in their effort to control territory. Size is also a useful distinguishing characteristic: Terrorist groups often consist of a small number of individuals, sometimes no more than a handful. Insurgent organizations like Hezbollah or the LTTE, in contrast, number in the thousands.

The definition does, however, exclude several types of groups that share many characteristics of insurgent movements. For example, internal paramilitary forces, such as the Autodefensas Unidas de Colombia (AUC) active in Colombia, do not share the above fundamental insurgent characteristics and therefore are not included in our analysis.[3] These internal forces have a territorial focus but are vigilante in nature and neither part of, nor involved in, underground political organizations. In many cases, their violence is simply backed by the state or its armed forces, either explicitly or implicitly. In addition, purely criminal groups, including large ones that regularly use violence, are excluded. Their goals are not tied to territorial control or even specifically to politics, except when needed to pro-

---

[2]For a review of different definitions of terrorism and the term's analytical murkiness in general, see Hoffman (1998), pp. 13–44.

[3]The AUC began as a constellation of drug-funded vigilante groups but increasingly developed a political agenda independent of narcotics trafficking.

mote criminal activities. Insurgent groups may traffic narcotics or other illicit enterprises, but these do not serve as rationales or goals for the organization. Rather, crime is a means to an end for insurgents (e.g., the generation of money to sustain operations), while for purely criminal groups such activities are ends in themselves. Furthermore, criminal groups usually do not seek to exert direct political control over a territory or populace as insurgents do. Some movements may begin as insurgencies and, over time, become criminal organizations as their political goals fade. Similarly, because insurgencies are ineluctably territorial-driven organizations, utopian movements and mystical cults such as the Aum Shinrikyo, whose objectives and self-identity transcend the bounds of territory, fall outside this definition. Finally, as alluded to above, movements that rely almost entirely on terrorism, such as the Basque separatist group ETA (Euskadi ta Askatasuna) and the November 17 group in Greece, are excluded.

METHODOLOGY

This report combines a broad survey of all major insurgencies active since 1991 (though many began years or even decades previously) with a more detailed, qualitative examination of several of the most-important insurgent movements active in the last decade to assess and analyze the phenomenon of post–Cold War external support for insurgencies. This combination of analytic methods has yielded a number of interesting findings. While the survey provided insight into the broad frequency of various phenomena, the case study approach proved particularly useful for making qualitative judgments about the impact of various types of support. The approaches together illustrate major trends in insurgency emerging from the last decade.

All the groups included in our review have inflicted in excess of 1,000 deaths per conflict. In addition, we examined certain insurgencies, such as the Slovene secession from the former Yugoslavia, that had a lower death toll but nonetheless "succeeded" because the movement in question took control of the government or gained a substantial degree of autonomy.

Although the above criteria appear clear, in practice they often required specific judgment calls with which other analysts might disagree. Among the ambiguities involving our selection and ordering of data were the following:

- Some insurgencies changed their names and, at times, their orientations, over the course of their struggle. Similarly, many insurgent movements split into rival factions at various points in their history. It would be possible to categorize them either as separate movements or as a single insurgency with different offshoots or phases. Our preference was to categorize these multiple organizations and names as a single insurgency to avoid giving the impression that many distinct insurgent groups existed when, in fact, only one was active.

- Some countries confronted several small insurgent groups that, together, had an impact disproportionate to their individual size and influence. Nonetheless, because these groups were demonstrably separate and independent entities and therefore, by themselves, were largely inconsequential, they did not meet the strict criteria given above. In the early 1990s, Afghanistan and Somalia, for example, had myriad small groups that fought quite fiercely, although the groups do not qualify for inclusion as an insurgency given these criteria. In such cases, we often amalgamated disparate organizations under one heading, even though these groups may even have fought with one another or otherwise did not consist of a single movement.

- The degree of territorial control of certain groups was often limited at best. The Provisional Irish Republican Army (PIRA) as well as the Iraqi-backed Mujahedin-e Khalq (MEK) both had territorial aspirations (and thus met the criteria in the definition), but their actual control was limited in duration and practice.

- At times, information on insurgent groups was severely limited. This was especially true for movements in Africa. Accordingly, several movements or manifestations of external support may require further elaboration as more information becomes available.

ORGANIZATION

The report has six remaining chapters. Chapter Two provides an overview of state support for insurgencies during the last decade, using the recent civil wars in the Congo to illustrate several of the more important arguments concerning the motivations of state supporters. Chapter Three examines the impact diasporas can play in supporting an insurgency, drawing on the example of the LTTE's successful use of Tamil migrant populations to sustain its overall struggle. Chapter Four assesses the role of refugees, analyzing the experience of the Taliban to show how, in certain circumstances, displaced communities may prove instrumental in an insurgent movement's success. Chapter Five briefly describes the contributions that a wide range of other non-state actors, such as religious organizations and other insurgent groups, can make. Chapter Six provides a more detailed analysis of the advantages of various types of outside support, elucidating when support is less useful and moreover, when it can reduce a movement's effectiveness. Chapter Seven concludes the report by presenting broader implications for insurgency analysis.

Chapter Two

STATE SUPPORT FOR INSURGENCIES

States remain among the most important, and most active, supporters of insurgent groups. Although diaspora communities, refugees,
and other non-state actors regularly provide assistance to rebel
groups in their home countries, the scale and range of backing that is
given is considerably less than that of states in most cases. This
chapter presents an overview of recent trends in state assistance to
insurgent movements. It reviews a wide range of guerrilla conflicts
active during the 1990s, noting both the frequency of state support
and qualitative judgments of its impact. Recent experiences of the
insurgencies in the Congo are then used to illustrate broader arguments about the importance and limits of state assistance. The
chapter concludes by assessing the motivations of state supporters,
drawing on both the Congo case study and other insurgencies' experiences.

STATE SUPPORT FOR INSURGENCIES IN THE 1990s:
AN OVERVIEW

State support has had a profound impact on the effectiveness of
many insurgencies since the end of the Cold War.[1] Of the 74 insurgencies reviewed here, state support played a significant or critical
role in 44 of them. The list of the insurgencies surveyed is presented

---

[1]Assessments of the impact of outside support are subjective. Although we have vet-
ted our judgments with a range of regional experts, it is possible that other analysts
may disagree with our judgments. We believe that the trends we identify are broad
enough that minor disagreements in coding would not significantly alter our conclusions.

9

in Appendix A. Table 2.1 offers our judgment of where government sponsorship played an important role in facilitating military, political, and logistical activities of a rebel movement. At times, the impact of state support was limited. Libya, for example, provided financial assistance to the Gerakan Aceh Merdeka in Indonesia, but this does not appear to have significantly helped the movement fight, recruit, or otherwise prosecute its struggle.

In many ways, the above overview underestimates the frequency of state support. In some instances, state support has not played a major role since 1991 but did play a crucial role in helping the movement survive and gain prominence during the 1980s. The LTTE, for example, received substantial Indian backing until 1987. Similarly, while Algeria did not provide significant assistance to the Polisario in Western Sahara during the 1990s, it did play a major role in sustaining this movement in its struggle against Morocco during the 1970s and 1980s.[2]

In general, state assistance helped rebel groups sustain their armed campaigns and improve their overall military and political effectiveness. Although guerrilla groups were rarely able to defeat organized armies on the battlefield, outside state support helped movements deprive their government adversaries of quick and easy victories. In many cases, this prolonged the conflict and increased the chance of a political settlement more favorable to the insurgents.

When judging the impact of state support, timing is essential. Assistance is usually most valuable early in a campaign, when it can prove central in establishing the insurgent group's viability and thus enhancing its longevity. Because the logistical requirements to create an insurgency are minimal or modest at best, even poor states can readily facilitate the emergence of a movement—although ensuring its ultimate success is considerably more difficult. Through the provision of sanctuary, arms, training, and money, governments have often played a critical role in augmenting an emergent group's resilience. State support is vital when the insurgent is facing a powerful enemy. Without some form of outside backing, usually and

---

[2]Lawless and Monahan (1987). In 1991, the United Nations (UN) brokered a cease-fire between Morocco and the Polisario, but many of the conditions have not been implemented.

Table 2.1

Insurgencies and Their State Supporters (1991–2000)

Country	Insurgency Name	Critical State Supporter	Significant State Supporter	Minor State Supporter
Afghanistan	Taliban	Pakistan		Saudi Arabia
Afghanistan	United Islamic Front for the Salvation of Afghanistan (UIFSA) or Northern Alliance	Iran, Russia, Uzbekistan		Tajikistan
Afghanistan	Various small movements based on ethnicity, tribe, region, or following an individual leader	Pakistan, Russia, Uzbekistan, Iran	Saudi Arabia	Tajikistan
Algeria	Islamic Salvation Army (AIS)			
Algeria	Armed Islamic Group (GIA)			
Angola	National Union for the Total Independence of Angola (UNITA)	South Africa, Tanzania, Zambia, Namibia		
Azerbaijan	Armenian separatists in Nagorno-Karbakh	Armenia, Russia		
Bosnia	Bosnian Croats	Croatia		
Bosnia	Bosnian Serbs	Serbia		
Burma	Karen National Union (KNU)			
Burundi	Conseil National pour la Defense et de Democratie (CNDD) and its armed wing, the Forces pour la Defense de la Democratie (FDD) and other ethnic Hutu groups		Tanzania	Congo

Table 2.1—continued

Country	Insurgency Name	Critical State Supporter	Significant State Supporter	Minor State Supporter
Cambodia	Khmer Rouge—Party of Democratic Kampuchea		China	Thailand
Colombia	National Liberation Army (ELN)			Venezuela, Cuba
Colombia	Revolutionary Armed Forces of Colombia (FARC)			Venezuela, Cuba
Croatia	Serb revolt in Krajina	Serbia		
Democratic Republic of the Congo	Pro-Kabila forces who defeated Mobutu Sese Seko	Rwanda, Uganda		Angola
Democratic Republic of the Congo	Rassemblement Congolais pour la Democratie (RCD-Kisangani)	Uganda		
Democratic Republic of the Congo	Rassemblement Congolais pour la Democratie (RCD-Goma)	Rwanda		
Democratic Republic of the Congo	Mouvement de Liberation Congolais (MLC)	Uganda		
Egypt	Gamaat Islamiya (IG) and other small Islamist groups			
Ethiopia	Oromo Liberation Front (OLF)		Eritrea, Somalia	
Georgia (Abkhazia)	Abkhaz separatists	Russia		

Table 2.1—continued

Country	Insurgency Name	Critical State Supporter	Significant State Supporter	Minor State Supporter
Georgia (South Ossetia)	South Ossetian separatists	Russia		
Guatemala	Various leftist groups			Cuba
Guinea Bissau	Antigovernment organizations			
India	United Liberation Front of Assam and other groups in Assam			Pakistan
India	National Front for the Liberation of Bodoland			Pakistan
India	Punjabi separatists	Pakistan		
India (Kashmir)	Hizb al Mujahideen	Pakistan		
India (Kashmir)	Harakat al-Ansar	Pakistan		
India (Kashmir)	Jammu and Kashmir Liberation Front (JKLF)	Pakistan		
India (Kashmir)	Lashkar-e-Taiba	Pakistan		
Indonesia	East Timor Guerrilla resistance			
Indonesia	Free Aceh Movement (GAM)			Libya
Iran	Mujahedin-e Khalq (MEK)	Iraq		Afghanistan
Iraq	Kurdistan Democratic Party (KDP)	Iran, U.S.		
Iraq	Patriotic Union of Kurdistan (PUK)	Iran, U.S.		
Iraq	Various Shi'a insurgents	Iran		U.S., Gulf state governments

Table 2.1—continued

Country	Insurgency Name	Critical State Supporter	Significant State Supporter	Minor State Supporter
Iraq	Iraqi National Congress (INC)	U.S.		
Israel (occupied territories)	Palestine Liberation Organization (PLO)	Various Arab states, wide political support		European governments, Russia, China, many others
Israel (occupied territories)	HAMAS		Iran, Gulf states	
Lebanon	Hezbollah	Syria, Iran		
Liberia	National Patriotic Front (NPFL) and associated factions (Charles Taylor)			Libya
Mexico	Zapatistas (or Ejercito Zapatista de Liberacion Nacional [EZLN])			
Moldova	Trans-Dniester guerrillas	Russia		
Mozambique	Mozambican National Resistance (RENAMO)	South Africa		
Nepal	Communist Party of Nepal—Maoist			
Pakistan	Mohajir Quami Movement (MQM)			India
Peru	Tupac Amaru Revolutionary Movement (MRTA)			
Peru	Sendero Luminoso			
Philippines	Moro Islamic Liberation Front (MILF)			Libya, Malaysia
Philippines	Moro National Liberation Front (MNLF)			

Table 2.1—continued

Country	Insurgency Name	Critical State Supporter	Significant State Supporter	Minor State Supporter
Republic of the Congo	Various opposition groups including the Pan-African Union for Social Democracy; the Congolese Movement for Democracy and Integral Development, and the Mouvement Congolais pour la Democratie et le Development Integral	Angola		
Russia	Chechen Rebels			
Rwanda	Rwandan Patriotic Front (RPF)	Uganda		
Rwanda	Forces Armees Rwandaises (ex-FAR)	Kabila government		
Senegal	Movement of Democratic Forces in the Casamance (MFDC)		Guinea Bissau	
Sierra Leone	Revolutionary United Front (RUF)	Liberia		Libya
South Africa	African National Congress (ANC)	Various frontline African states		European governments, Russia, China, many others
Sri Lanka	Liberation Tigers of Tamil Eelam (LTTE)			
Sudan	South Sudan Independence Movement/Army (SSIM/A)			
Sudan	National Democratic Alliance—comprises several opposition organizations, of which Sudan People's Liberation Movement is the largest			

Table 2.1—continued

Country	Insurgency Name	Critical State Supporter	Significant State Supporter	Minor State Supporter
Tajikistan	United Tajik Opposition			
Tajikistan	Pro-CIS forces	Russia, Uzbekistan		
Thailand	Pattani United Liberation Organization (PULO)		Malaysia	
Turkey	Kurdish Workers Party (PKK)	Syria, Iraq		Iran, Iraq, Greece
Uganda	Allied Democratic Forces (ADF)			Zaire, Congo
Uganda	Lord's Resistance Army (LRA)		Sudan	Zaire, Congo
United Kingdom	Provisional Irish Republican Army			
Uzbekistan	Islamic Movement of Uzbekistan (IMU)			
Western Sahara	Polisario Front		Algeria	
Yugoslavia (Former)	Kosovo Liberation Army (KLA)	U.S. and NATO allies		
Yugoslavia (Former)	Slovene secessionists			
Yugoslavia (Former)	Croatian secessionists			

most critically in the form of sanctuary, an insurgent movement risks being crushed before it has a chance to organize and make even minimal inroads. Thus, providing the same amount of arms, money, or other assistance is likely to have a far greater impact on a fledgling insurgency than a fully developed one.

WHERE STATE SUPPORT OCCURS

State support is neither specifically linked to one part of the world, to a particular type of insurgency, nor to any specific country or cause. In Asia, Africa, Europe, and the Middle East, governments have supported rebel groups. However, since the end of the Cold War, the overall incidence of insurgencies in Latin America, and accordingly of outside support, has diminished. This decline in both the number of insurgencies and in government sponsorship may reflect the ideological nature of many movements in that region. Also following 1991, many of the insurgencies driven largely by Marxist ideology, such as several movements in Peru and Central America, have often collapsed, while those more religious or ethnic in nature have often survived or even prospered.[3]

In the absence of superpower rivalry, insurgencies today must look for other sources of support. Most often this support is provided by local governments that border the country in which a group is fighting. Although countries as diverse as Libya, Iran, and the United States have aided rebels far from their borders, state support is primarily a local rather than international phenomenon. With a decline in superpower involvement also came a decline in the scale of assistance. The United States provided billions of dollars to the Afghan mujahedin and hundreds of millions of dollars to the Nicaraguan contras. By comparison, most state supporters now lack the tremendous resources that Washington and Moscow lavished on their insurgent proxies during the Cold War. Pakistan, one of the most generous sponsors of insurgent groups in the 1990s, provided tens of millions of dollars to its favored movements.

_____

[3]Byman and Van Evera (1998), pp. 41–43. The Revolutionary Armed Forces of Colombia (FARC), of course, remains an important exception to this generalization about Latin America.

STATE SUPPORTERS AND THE DEMOCRATIC REPUBLIC OF THE CONGO

Although the scale and scope of state assistance has dropped since the end of the Cold War, government backing for an insurgent group can still have a decisive impact. The experience of the Democratic Republic of the Congo, formerly known as Zaire, illustrates this tremendous potential.

The origins of the contemporary crisis in the Congo date back to 1996 when Rwanda and Uganda intervened to overthrow Mobutu Sese Seko—the president of Zaire—and replace him with a protégé of their own, Laurent Kabila. Kabila had long struggled against the Mobutu regime, but he commanded little support inside Zaire. It was not until he received significant outside backing that he was able to overwhelm the existing government. On the one hand, Rwanda sought to eliminate the remnants of the Hutu militias (the *interahamwe*) that had carried out the 1994 genocide in Rwanda and which continued to be supported by Mobutu in Zaire. In addition, Rwanda sought to protect the minority Tutsi population in eastern Congo from attacks both by the interahamwe and a local pro-Hutu tribal militia, the Mai Mai. On the other hand, Uganda sought to secure its western frontier and to prevent hostile guerrilla groups such as the Allied Democratic Forces (ADF) and the Lords Resistance Army (LRA) from using bases in eastern Congo to stage cross-border attacks (see *IISS Strategic Comments*, 1999, p. 2; Lemarchand, 1999, p. 196; Odera, 1998, pp. 47–56; *New York Times*, 1997). Other neighbors of Zaire, such as Angola, also supported the effort to topple Mobutu because of his support for dissidents and insurgencies that sought to overthrow their governments.

As soon as he was placed in power, however, Kabila turned against his former patrons. Not only did he increasingly criticize the influence of Uganda and, in particular, Rwanda in the newly liberated country's administration, but, in an act of astounding treachery, he allied himself with the same Hutu militias that were formerly supported by Mobutu and against whom he had been fighting. In addition, Kabila made no attempt to prevent the ADF from using eastern Congo as a haven from which to launch attacks into Uganda. In response, the Ugandan and Rwandan regimes united in armed support for a new rebel alliance, the Congolese Rally for Democracy

(CRD), with Kampala establishing a second organization, the Movement for the Liberation of the Congo (MLC) to further bolster its position (see Gourevitch, 2000, pp. 55–56; Lemarchand, 1999, p. 200; *Washington Post,* 2000a; *The Economist,* 1999; *New York Times,* 1997).

The anti-Kabila effort led to a far greater struggle that, in turn, engulfed much of central Africa. Both Zimbabwe and Angola[4] were drawn into the conflict, hoping to stabilize the Congo under Kabila. These regimes also helped themselves to the Congo's considerable diamond wealth.[5] In addition, a growing divergence of opinion over the purpose of military involvement in the Congo, combined with Rwandan claims of high-level corruption within the Ugandan army, led to increasing Kigali-Kampala tensions that finally exploded into violence in August 1999 (Gourevitch, 2000, p. 61). This rift among the two former allies contributed to the split in their insurgent proxy in the Congo. The CRD divided into two movements: a main CRD-Goma faction that continues to be supported by Rwanda and a smaller splinter organization, the CRD–Liberation Movement (CRD-ML), which receives the backing of Kampala. The complexities of the situation, and the complicated entanglements that it has spawned, have aptly been described by one commentator as a Lewis Carroll–like "portmanteau war," involving a host of conflicts, all having their own dynamic, yet simultaneously remaining closely intertwined with one another (Gourevitch, 2000, p. 57).

---

[4]Namibia also has a limited presence in the Congo. Its influence is marginal, however, serving mainly as a symbolic show of support for Zimbabwe.

[5]By far the biggest diamond prize in the Congo is the deposit near the city of Mbuji Mayi, 1,000 miles southwest of Kisangani. There are rumors that Harare will be paid with proceeds from the controversial Oryx Diamonds Company, which is currently seeking a listing on the London Stock Exchange. The allegations have come in the wake of Oryx's reverse takeover of another London-listed company, Petra Diamonds Ltd. Sources close to this latter deal claim that a shadowy, Zimbabwean-run military company known as Osleg will receive a guaranteed 40 percent of the profits in this $1 billion diamond venture and is under no obligation to make any financial outlay to the project. For further details see *Zimbabwe Independent* (2000); Harden (2000); and *IISS Strategic Comments* (1999), p. 1.

THE BENEFITS OF STATE SUPPORT

The two main insurgent groups in the Congo—the MLC and the CRD (both Goma and Kisangani factions)[6]—owe much of their existence and subsequent survival to support from Uganda and Rwanda.

Indeed, because these insurgencies appear to lack significant popular support at home and command few resources, outside support was initially necessary to make them credible opponents of the government. Outside powers kept rivalries among local warlords in check. Should outsiders become less involved, these insurgent groups may fracture. In addition, because the factions have little ideological strength or a strong popular base, many fighters would most likely switch to the government side if offered even minor concessions.

The MLC, created in November 1998 and led by Jean-Pierre Bemba, is armed, trained, and financed by Uganda and operates primarily in northwest Congo. It has gained considerable control over this territory and is currently seeking to expand further south to the junction between the Ubangi and Congo rivers. From there, the rebels hope to proceed to their ultimate objective—Kinshasa, the Congolese capital (*IISS Strategic Comments,* 1999, p. 2; *The Economist,* 1999; McNeil, 1999; *Washington Post,* 2000a).

The CRD was established as a Rwandan and Ugandan proxy on August 16, 1998. Although originally created as a unified alliance, it has since split into two competing factions, mirroring the wider rift in relations between Rwanda and Kampala. The smaller of the two groups is the Ugandan-backed CRD-ML, which is led by Ernest Wamba dia Wamba. The larger and more powerful faction (and the one with which this section is concerned), the Rwandan-supported CRD-Goma, exists as the main rebel grouping in northeast Congo,

---

[6]In addition to these organizations, several other Congolese rebel groups exist. Among the more important are the Republican Federalist Forces of Joseph Mutambo, which has been identified with a dissident Banyamulenge faction in South Kivu; the Mai Mai, a local anti-Banyamulenge, anti-Tutsi militia reportedly led by Charles Simba; dissident units of the former Armed Forces of Zaire; ex-members of the (Hutu) Armed Forces of Rwanda; the Public Salvation Army, a shadowy, anti-Kabila group that first emerged in April 2000; and local Hema and Lendu tribal armies in the forested highlands above Lake Albert in northeast Congo. See Adeyemi (2000), p. 40; and Kizito (1999).

where it enjoys the run of the land. A combined leadership oversees the organization, consisting of a president, Emile Ilungo; a first vice president, Jean-Pierre Ondekane; and a military commander, Hugo Ilondo (Adeyemi, 2000, p. 39; *Agence Presse France*, 2000; Lemarchand, 1999, p. 200; *IISS Strategic Comments*, 1999, p. 2; McNeil, 1999; *Washington Post*, 2000a). The troika's overall aim is to expand southwest and, like the MLC, seize control of Kinshasa.[7]

Both the MLC and the two CRD factions suffer from poor morale and are comprised of unskilled and undisciplined fighters. Without large numbers of troops from Uganda and Rwanda to leaven their forces, the fighting power of these insurgent groups would be limited at best; indeed, both movements would probably degenerate into undisciplined bands of brigands.

Rwanda has many objectives in supporting the CRD. Most important, it seeks to ensure a friendly government in Kinshasa in order to crush the remnants of the Hutu interahamwe and their supporters responsible for the 1994 genocide in Rwanda. When Kabila began supporting anti-Tutsi groups, the objective of overthrowing him, or at least destabilizing his regime, became imperative. Assisting the Congo's *banyamulenge*, a people with ties to the Tutsis, gained greater importance as the Kabila regime and Hutu marauders began to target them. Sometimes the effort to overthrow Kabila also assumed a strong personal element of outrage, as officials in Kigali recoiled from what they saw as Kabila's betrayal of their support. More broadly, Kigali has sought to ensure its influence in order to prevent renewed raids from the Congo into Rwanda. Once it became clear that an outright victory was not within its grasp, Rwanda sought instead to ensure its influence over various opposition groups, particularly those near its border, and to keep the Kinshasa regime weak. Thus it has continued to provide a wide range of support to the CRD-Goma, even though it remains insufficient to gain an outright victory.

Rwanda uses its proxy to further its agenda not only in the Congo, but elsewhere in central Africa.[8] The CRD-Goma allows the ADF to

---

[7]Personal correspondence with Central Africa regional expert, United Kingdom, October, 2000. See also *Agence Presse France* (2000).

[8]On the negative side, seeking to support external insurgencies has brought rebel groups of the Congo into conflict with what might otherwise have been important and

operate more or less freely and has made no move to prevent the force from using the northeastern border regions as a base from which to stage attacks into neighboring Uganda. This tacit support, though not officially acknowledged, is almost certainly a product of Rwanda's wider conflict with Kampala. The CRD-Goma remains heavily dependent on Rwanda's backing and therefore has an active interest in allying itself with Rwanda's current anti-Museveni agenda.[9] Moreover, supporting the ADF in its struggle against Kampala presumably facilitates Ilungo's, Ilondo's, and Ondekane's own internal struggles against Wamba dia Wamba's faction, which remains oriented toward Uganda (see Adeyemi, 2000, p. 40).

Uganda's support for the CRD-ML and the MLC follows both similar and different lines. Like Rwanda, Kampala seeks to preserve influence over its large and important neighbor and to prevent the Congo from being used by antigovernment insurgents. Uganda's leaders also share Rwanda's outrage over Kabila's betrayal and have not hesitated to use their two proxies to plunder the Congo's mineral wealth, thereby enriching individuals within the government and military.

The Ugandan and Rwandan intervention also provoked a counterbalancing reaction by the Congo's other neighbors. Almost all of the Congo's neighbors supported, at least tacitly, the effort to oust Mobutu. However, the subsequent anti-Kabila movement raised fears that Uganda and Rwanda wanted to create a puppet state within the Congo. Angola and Zimbabwe in particular opposed the effort to replace Kabila.[10] The timely intervention of their forces prevented Rwandan troops, acting ostensibly in the name of the CRD, from seizing the capital. Their subsequent support for Kabila

---

useful state backers. For example, MLC contacts with the National Union for the Total Independence of Angola (UNITA) have cost the group diplomatically. While Paris has expressed sympathy toward Bemba's agenda, it remains acutely sensitive to any actions that could unduly undermine bilateral Angolan-French relations. Broadening the conflict has also increased support for Kabila's government and for other opponents of the insurgent movements, making their ultimate aim more difficult to achieve. Personal correspondence with Central Africa regional expert, United Kingdom, October 2000.

[9]Personal correspondence with Central Africa regional expert, United Kingdom, October 2000.

[10]Namibia also contributed to the defense of Kabila, but its role was marginal.

was instrumental in offsetting Uganda's and Rwanda's support of the CRD and the MLC; their troops continue to provide a backbone to the Congo's otherwise-worthless military forces.[11]

MOTIVATIONS OF STATE SUPPORTERS

As the case of the Congo illustrates, states support insurgent movements for a variety of reasons, many of which overlap. The most common motivations are outlined in Table 2.2 and are discussed in more detail below.[12] The table indicates that states are primarily motivated by geopolitics rather than ideology, ethnic affinity, or religious sentiment. Although these less strategic rationales sometimes play an important role in regimes' decisions to back insurgencies, they are far-less-frequent motivators than those involving considerations of regional influence and strategic competition. Indeed, when ethnic kin or religious brethren do receive support, it is often done to further realpolitik ambitions as opposed to being an end itself. Ethnic and religious justifications are often mere window dressing.

Regional Influence

Governments frequently support insurgents to increase local or regional influence, particularly along their borders, and especially as a means of applying pressure on a rival. Though the Congo is perhaps the most obvious example of a situation where neighboring states have backed insurgents (or a weak state) to extend their influ-

---

[11]In January 2001, Kabila was killed in an apparent dispute with a bodyguard. His son, Joseph Kabila, assumed power. Whether he is a mere figurehead is not yet known. At the time of this writing, Angola and Zimbabwe were both exhibiting increased weariness with the war in the Congo because of its economic toll; they have hinted of an increased willingness to withdraw their troops from the country.

[12]In rare cases, personal reasons also lead leaders to support insurgents abroad. The Doe government in Liberia killed relatives of the leaders of Burkina Faso and the Ivory Coast, leading them to aid Libya in its backing of Charles Taylor's movement.

Table 2.2

State Supporter Motivations

Country	Insurgency Name	Supportg. States[a]	Reg. Inf.	Destb. Neigh.	Pay-back	Reg. Ch.	Infl. Op.	Intl. Sec.	Pres-tige	Supt. Co-Relig.	Supt. Co-Eth.	Irre-dent.	Leftist Ideol.	Plun-der
Afghanistan	Various small movements based on ethnicity, tribe, region, or individual leader	Pakistan, Iran, Russia, Uzbekistan, Saudi Arabia	X	X			X			X	X			
Afghanistan	United Islamic Front for the Salvation of Afghanistan (UIFSA) or Northern Alliance	Iran, Russia, Uzbekistan	X	X	X		X			X	X			
Afghanistan	Taliban	Pakistan	X	X	X	X	X	X	X	X	X			
Angola	National Union for the Total Independence of Angola (UNITA)	South Africa, Tanzania, Zambia, Namibia	X	X	X	X	X	X	X					X

Table 2.2—continued

Country	Insurgency Name	Supportg. States [a]	Reg. Inf.	Destb. Neigh.	Pay-back	Reg. Ch.	Infl. Op.	Intl. Sec.	Pres-tige	Supt. Co-Relig.	Supt. Co-Eth.	Irre-dent.	Leftist Ideol.	Plun-der
Azerbaijan	Armenian separatists in Nagorno-Karbakh	Armenia, Russia	X								X			
Bosnia	Bosnian Serbs	Serbia	X				X	X			X	X		
Bosnia	Bosnian Croats	Croatia	X					X			X	X		
Burundi	Ethnic Hutu groups	Tanzania	X					X						
Cambodia	Khmer Rouge—Party of Democratic Kampuchea	China	X			X								
Croatia	Serb revolt in Krajina	Serbia	X								X	X		
Democratic Republic of the Congo	Pro-Kabila forces who defeated Mobutu Sese Seko	Uganda, Rwanda	X		X	X		X			X			
Democratic Republic of the Congo	Rassemblement Congolais pour la Democratie (RCD-Kisangani)	Uganda	X		X	X	X							X

Table 2.2—continued

Country	Insurgency Name	Supportg, States[a]	Reg, Inf.	Destb. Neigh.	Pay-back	Reg, Ch.	Infl. Op.	Intl. Sec.	Pres-tige	Supt. Co-Relig.	Supt. Co-Eth.	Irre-dent.	Leftist Ideol.	Plun-der
Democratic Republic of the Congo	Rassemblement Congolais pour la Democratie (RCD-Goma)	Rwanda	X		X	X	X	X			X			X
Democratic Republic of the Congo	Mouvement de Liberation Congolais (MLC)	Uganda	X		X	X	X							
Ethiopia	Oromo Liberation Front (OLF)	Eritrea, Somalia	X	X								X		
Georgia	Abkhaz separatists	Russia	X	X	X				X					
Georgia	South Ossetian separatists	Russia	X	X	X				X				X	
India	Punjabi separatists	Pakistan	X	X										
India (Kashmir)	Lashkar-e-Taiba	Pakistan	X	X			X	X		X		X		
India (Kashmir)	Harkat al-Ansar	Pakistan	X	X			X	X		X		X		
India (Kashmir)	Hizb al Mujahideen	Pakistan	X	X			X	X		X		X		

Table 2.2—continued

Country	Insurgency Name	Supportg. States[a]	Reg. Inf.	Destb. Neigh.	Pay-back	Reg. Ch.	Infl. Op.	Intl. Sec.	Pres-tige	Supt. Co-Relig.	Supt. Co-Eth.	Irre-dent.	Leftist Ideol.	Plun-der
India (Kashmir)	Jammu and Kashmir Liberation Front (JKLF)	Pakistan	X	X									X	
Iran	Mujahedin-e Khalq (MEK)	Iraq	X	X	X									
Iraq	Iraqi National Congress (INC)	U.S.	X	X		X	X							
Iraq	Patriotic Union of Kurdistan (PUK)	Iran, U.S.	X	X	X		X	X						
Iraq	Kurdistan Democratic Party (KDP)	Iran, U.S.	X	X	X		X	X						
Iraq	Various Shi'a insurgents	Iran	X	X	X	X	X	X	X	X				
Israel (occup. territories)	HAMAS	Iran, Gulf states	X	X		X	X		X	X				
Israel (occup. territories)	Palestine Liberation Organization (PLO)	Various Arab states	X	X		X	X		X		X			

Table 2.2—continued

Country	Insurgency Name	Supportg. States [a]	Reg. Inf.	Destb. Neigh.	Pay-back	Reg. Ch.	Infl. Op.	Intl. Sec.	Pres-tige	Supt. Co-Relig.	Supt. Co-Eth.	Irre-dent.	Leftist Ideol.	Plun-der
Lebanon	Hezbollah	Iran, Syria	X			X	X		X	X	X			
Moldova	Trans-Dniester guerrillas	Russia	X						X		X			
Mozambique	Mozambican National Resistance (RENAMO)	South Africa	X	X	X	X		X						
Republic of the Congo	Various opposition groups (e.g. the Pan-African Union for Social Democracy; the Congolese Movement)	Angola	X											
Rwanda	Rwandan Patriotic Front (RPF)	Uganda	X			X	X	X						

Table 2.2—continued

Country	Insurgency Name	Supportg. States[a]	Reg. Inf.	Destb. Neigh.	Pay-back	Reg. Ch.	Infl. Op.	Intl. Sec.	Pres-tige	Supt. Co-Relig.	Supt. Co-Eth.	Irre-dent.	Leftist Ideol.	Plun-der
Rwanda	Forces Armees Rwandaises (ex-FAR)	Kabila gov't in the Congo		X				X						
Senegal	Movement of Democratic Forces in the Casamance (MFDC)	Guinea Bissau	X	X										
Sierra Leone	Revolutionary United Front (RUF)	Liberia under Taylor	X	X	X	X			X					X
South Africa	African National Congress (ANC)	Frontline African states	X	X		X					X		X	
Tajikistan	pro-CIS forces	Russia, Uzbekistan	X			X			X		X			
Thailand	Pattani United Liberation Organization (PULO)	Malaysia	X	X						X	X			
Turkey	Kurdish Workers Party (PKK)	Syria, Iraq	X	X										

Table 2.2—continued

Country	Insurgency Name	Supportg. States[a]	Reg. Inf.	Destb. Neigh.	Pay-back	Reg. Ch.	Infl. Op.	Intl. Sec.	Pres-tige	Supt. Co-Relig.	Supt. Co-Eth.	Irre-dent.	Leftist Ideol.	Plun-der
Uganda	Lord's Resistance Army (LRA)	Sudan	X	X	X									
Western Sahara	Polisario Front	Algeria	X										X	
Yugoslavia (Former)	Kosovo Liberation Army (KLA)	U.S. and NATO allies	X			X								

[a]Crucial or significant support only; the motivations of minor state supporters are not included in this list.

NOTE: Abbreviations in the headings signify (from left to right): Regional Influence, Destabilize Neighbors, Payback, Regime Change, Ensuring Influence Within the Opposition, Internal Security, Prestige, Support Coreligionists, Support Co-Ethnics, Irredentism, Leftist Ideology, and Plunder. For further explanation, see the corresponding sections in this chapter.

ence, it is also a common feature of many guerrilla conflicts elsewhere. Russia, for example, has abetted movements throughout the former Soviet Union in an attempt to ensure its hegemony in the so-called "near abroad." Such assistance has borne tangible benefits. Georgia, Moldova, and Tajikistan, for instance, are all now far more sensitive to Moscow's concerns as a result of Russian-backed insurgencies in each of these countries. Similarly, Pakistan has supported a range of groups in Kashmir and Bangladesh, as well as the Taliban in Afghanistan, in order to increase its influence along its southern border with India and gain leverage over its larger and more powerful neighbor.

Often a state uses an insurgency as a bargaining chip to increase its influence over a rival. The Persian Gulf provides a good example of this. Iran supports the Supreme Assembly for the Islamic Revolution in Iraq (SAIRI), while Iraq backs the anti-Tehran MEK, as part of their ongoing regional bilateral competition. Indeed, the insurgent operations of these two groups have become a revealing barometer of wider regional tensions. When Iraqi-Iranian relations are improved, the volume of rebel activity tends to decline; when they are tense, the level of violence often rises.

This shift in motivations from international to local rivalries represents a major change from the end of the Cold War. Although the United States has backed antigovernment rebels in Iraq to ensure its influence in the critical Gulf region, Washington relies far less on surrogates as instruments of foreign policy than it did during the Cold War. The same is true for Russia and China; even when these powers support insurgents, they do so locally, not internationally. (This generalization is not absolute.) Lesser powers with greater ambitions may at times support insurgencies to project influence outside their immediate regions. France, for example, has supported guerrilla movements fighting English-speaking governments in Africa in order to preserve its standing among Francophone Africans.[13] Similarly, Tehran's support for the Lebanese Hezbollah and Palestinian HAMAS has provided it with a voice in the Palestinian-Israeli peace negotiations that it would not otherwise have, endowing it with a

---

[13]Some analysts argue that France has developed commercial relations with Taylor and the National Patriotic Front of Liberia (NPFL) in part to offset growing Anglophone dominance in western Africa.

significant role in Islamic issues. Nevertheless, France and Iran's efforts are exceptions to the general post–Cold War increase of local compared to international rivalries as motivations for states to support insurgent movements.

Destabilize Neighbors

For some states, insurgencies are essentially war by other means. Support to rebel movements is therefore seen as an alternative and a less-direct means of weakening and undermining enemies or rivals. In the Congo today, both Rwanda and Uganda appear to recognize that while an outright victory is not likely, they can, however, continue to support the MLC and the CRD as a way of destabilizing a hostile regime. India and Pakistan have backed insurgents in each other's territory throughout their decades-long rivalry. Uzbekistan, Russia, and Iran—all share an enmity for Afghanistan's Taliban—similarly have cooperated by supporting the anti-Taliban Northern Alliance (NA).

Using an insurgency to destabilize a neighbor can be effective. For most states, ensuring domestic stability is a top priority; any threat to the prevailing social order commands immediate attention (Ayoob, 1991, pp. 257–283; David, 1991). At the very least, the targeted state will have to expend considerable resources to contain rebel movements fighting within its territory; by contrast, the opposing guerrilla groups typically require only a small number of fighters and arms to remain active.[14] India, for example, maintains several hundred thousand paramilitary, police, and army forces to suppress the estimated 3,500 militants fighting in Jammu and Kashmir.[15] In addition to tying down large numbers of troops, fighting an insurgency often

---

[14]The true size of a deployment depends primarily on the total size of a population, not on the total size of the guerrilla movement. When violence is common, the ratio of police force to total population becomes quite high. In Punjab, for example, the Indian government had a security force of about 115,000 in a territory of roughly 20.2 million—a force ratio of 5.7 per thousand. The British reached a level of 20 per thousand in the Malay insurgency in the 1950s, and in Northern Ireland this level reached around 20 per thousand as well (Quinlivan, 1995–1996, pp. 59–69, see especially pp. 60–64).

[15]Indian sources claim the figure is roughly 200,000 troops, but other informed observers say it may run as high as 500,000.

adversely affects the morale of government forces, particularly when their training emphasizes conventional war-fighting (Schofield, 2000, pp. 168–169).

If the insurgency grows and becomes increasingly protracted and formidable, the movement can weaken a state economically. Israel and Egypt, for example, have lost billions of dollars in tourism because of violence perpetrated by Palestinian guerrillas and Gama-a-Islamiya and Islamic Jihad radicals, respectively. Similarly, the Sudan has long been prevented from developing its oil and agricultural sectors largely because the ongoing war against the Sudan Peoples Liberation Army has discouraged outside investment and prevented the government from developing productive capabilities.

Regime Change

States sometimes use insurgents to overthrow a rival government.[16] Uganda and Rwanda's backing of Kabila to overthrow Mobutu is a notable case in point. The two governments' subsequent efforts to depose the surprisingly ungrateful Kabila, while less successful, were motivated by the same objective. Similar examples abound elsewhere. Pakistan used the Taliban to topple the Rabbani government in Kabul, Russia ousted the United Tajik Opposition–led government in Tajikistan, and the United States has tried to use Iraqi oppositionists to overthrow the Baath regime in Iraq.

In general, using a proxy movement to topple another government is exceptionally difficult. While maintaining a viable insurgency requires considerable effort—particularly if the opposing state is strong—deposing that government often requires an exponential increase in the scale and scope of support provided because of fundamental asymmetries in manpower and arms. Rival governments may also come to rescue the threatened regime or even sponsor rival insurgencies of their own. Because regime change is difficult, outside governments often lower their expectations and settle for weak-

---

[16]Many regimes, of course, would prefer to have the insurgents in power rather than the existing government. However, many governments provide only limited support to insurgents and do not use the movement as part of an overall regime-change strategy.

ening a rival and otherwise extending their influence. For example, when Rwanda tried to support the CRD in its bid to replace Kabila, Angola and other states intervened on Kinshasa's side to protect their own interests. Kigali then settled for a strategy aimed at undermining, if not fully removing, Kabila from power.

Insurgent movements that come to power, however, are not always pawns of their sponsors. The Congo, again, supports this case. Although Kabila initially acted as Rwanda's proxy in unseating Mobutu, he soon recognized that in order to consolidate power and build his domestic legitimacy he would have to distance himself from his foreign state sponsor. It was for this reason that Rwanda subsequently backed the CRD.

Payback

External backing of an insurgency often creates chain reactions, where one state's support for a guerrilla group leads its adversary to provide assistance to the other country's enemies. Angola, Zimbabwe, and Uganda all joined Rwanda's effort to overthrow Mobutu because the Zairian dictator had allowed a number of insurgent groups to operate from his country's soil. Similarly, anti-government Sudanese groups have received support from Khartoum's neighbors largely because Sudan has backed local insurgencies elsewhere.

Concern about payback can also act to restrain government intervention. Indeed, many governments around the world that have restive minorities or other potential dissidents remain concerned that an aggressive policy abroad may lead rivals to foment discontent at home. Iran, for example, was willing to forgo opportunities to extend its regional influence by supporting coreligionists in Central Asia and the Caucasus mostly out of fear that other states would do the same to Iran.

Ensuring Influence Within the Opposition

At times, states may intervene in a neighboring country simply to ensure that the opposition movement does not adopt goals or policies hostile to its interests. Uganda, for example, lacks Rwanda's overriding concern about guerrillas operating from the Congo (although it does worry about the ADF and the LRA). However, it has supported its own resistance factions in order to ensure that the resistance is not completely subordinate to Kigali. States may also seek to change the ultimate goals of an insurgency. Pakistan, for example, has championed Islamic insurgencies in Kashmir to the detriment of long-standing nationalist groups such as the Jammu and Kashmir Liberation Front (JKLF). Although support for the once-popular JKLF might have proved an even bigger thorn in India's side than the various Islamic groups that Pakistan currently backs, Islamabad preferred to aid those insurgents whose agendas squared more directly with its own goals.

States may also seek to work with their own proxies to undercut rival governments that support other insurgencies. Uganda and Rwanda, for example, split the anti-Kabila CRD movement into hostile fragments as part of their interstate rivalry, preferring a weaker opposition to one that might become independent or dominated by a single government. Similarly, during the Lebanese civil war, Israel, Iraq, Syria, and Iran each supported one or more Lebanese factions in order to counter the influence of state rivals.

Internal Security

Sometimes state sponsors will use insurgents against their own dissidents or other antigovernment groups. Kigali supported Kabila and, later, the CRD in an effort to crush surviving Hutu interahamwe who were staging attacks from the Congo into Rwanda, while Uganda worked with its proxies to shut down the LRA and the ADF. Iran has similarly used Iraqi Kurdish groups to attack MEK fighters based inside Iraq. Geography and proximity clearly play a key role: The insurgents must be able to operate freely enough to attack dissidents or otherwise aid their sponsor.

Governments may also support insurgents to pacify refugees and displaced migrants in their own country, and provide an external outlet for their frustrations. Kampala's support for the RPF occurred in part to prevent unrest among the large group of Tutsis who had fled to Uganda. Similarly, Lebanon allowed the PLO tremendous autonomy during the 1970s to avoid turning the large, well-armed

Palestinian community against what was then a fragmented and weak regime.

Prestige

A regime's prestige may grow from supporting an insurgency. This motivation is particularly important if the leader or regime has ambitions outside its immediate neighborhood. Iran has aided Islamic groups, particularly the Lebanese Hezbollah, in part to burnish its credentials as the champion of the Muslim faithful. Libya has sought to enhance its image as a leading revolutionary state by aiding insurgents in the Philippines, Indonesia, and western Africa. Similarly, many Arab states provided support to the PLO to strengthen their Arab nationalist credentials.

Support Coreligionists

Religion can be a powerful motivation for states to support insurgencies. Iran, for example, has backed Shi'a coreligionists in Iraq, Lebanon, Bahrain, Kuwait, Saudi Arabia, and Bosnia (and most likely elsewhere) in part because of its commitment to exporting militant Islam. One benefit Pakistan gains from fomenting unrest in Afghanistan and Kashmir is the prestige derived from championing Islam, a benefit of growing importance for Islamabad given the importance of political Islam in Pakistan today (Stern, 2000, pp. 115–126).

In general, however, state support for insurgencies based on religious ties has declined since the end of the Cold War. Iran, known for a while as the staunchest and most active champion of radical Muslim groups, has reduced both the scope and scale of its support in recent years.[17] Similarly Sudan, while still maintaining ties to several groups, has focused more on ensuring order at home and gaining the goodwill of its neighbors. This decline, however, should

---

[17]During the 1980s, Iran supported a host of Islamist groups, particularly Shi'a groups, and provided them with a wide range of arms, training, and other forms of support. This backing declined in the 1990s, although ties to Sunni Arab groups increased. After the election of President Khatami in 1997, ties to militant groups, while still frequent, decreased in intensity and frequency.

not be overstated. Although absolute numbers suggest state support to revolutionary Islam has declined, some of the most serious insurgencies in the world today continue to be backed by Muslim governments.

Acquiescence rather than active assistance may also act as a form of assistance given to other Islamic insurgencies. Riyadh, for example, does not have extensive state-to-state contacts with many radical Islamic groups. However, it has long allowed its wealthy citizens to aid radical movements—such as HAMAS, the Taliban, various Kashmiri groups, and other extremists—with little interference.

Support Co-Ethnics

State support for ethnic kin abroad was relatively common during the 1990s. Rwanda's intervention in the Congo occurred in part to aid the banyamulenge against regime and Hutu repression. Following the collapse of the Soviet Union, Uzbekistan supported Uzbeks in Afghanistan, Armenia supported Armenians in Azerbaijan, and Russia supported ethnic Russians in Moldova.

Support of this kind often represents a convenient pretext for intervention that is in fact frequently undertaken for geopolitical reasons. Russia, for example, has used the potential plight of Russian speakers in its former empire to justify military support for insurgents operating in Moldova and Tajikistan in order to continue its influence in the "near abroad."

Domestic politics is also an important reason states support co-ethnics. Governments often emphasize their defense of ethnic brethren abroad to burnish their nationalist credentials with audiences at home. When co-ethnics are oppressed, killed, or displaced, governments are likely to come under tremendous pressure from sympathetic citizens to respond. Arab governments, for example, support the Palestinian cause despite their many disagreements with the Arafat-dominated leadership because any significant reduction in ties, much less a complete break, would certainly be opposed by their own citizens.

Irredentism

Outright irredentism, while rare, may also motivate states to support insurgencies. In general, governments in heterogeneous states fear that adding additional territory and populations will upset existing ethnic balances.[18] However, more-homogenous states may be more inclined to acquire territory that is home to the same ethnic group. After the collapse of central authority in Yugoslavia, both Serbia and Croatia sought to annex parts of Bosnia-Herzegovina. Armenia also attempted to expand its borders after the fall of the Soviet Union, while Pakistan has used Islamic insurgencies in Kashmir to press its claim for the divided territory.

These instances of open irredentism all occurred in response to the collapse of central authority in an existing multiethnic state. When the Ottoman, Yugoslav, British, and Russian empires were strong, the equation of provincial boundaries with national populations had little value or meaning. Indeed, imperial governments deliberately sought to weaken national consciousness and political strength by geographically separating groups for administrative purposes. When imperial rule ended, however, artificially drawn boundaries became disputed state borders. Minorities in a large multiethnic empire became one of two or three groups in a much smaller state. Groups suddenly found themselves part of a rival nation's real or perceived ethnic homeland, increasing the chance that they would suffer discrimination or even expulsion (Byman and Van Evera, 1998, pp. 25–30). Serbs in Bosnia, for example, went from being part of Yugoslavia's dominant community to members of a second-class minority when the federation began to break apart. As such, they eagerly supported efforts by Belgrade to reclaim much of Bosnia-Herzegovina. Such actors have proven to be convenient vehicles for regimes seeking to redraw their frontiers.

---

[18]Horowitz (1985), pp. 281–288. Paul Huth (1996, p. 81) argues that a state's linguistic or cultural ties to parts of a neighbor's population has little impact on the frequency of territorial disputes.

Leftist Ideology

Although nonreligious ideologically based movements are common in several parts of the world, the driving forces of communism and anticommunism rarely motivate states to support an insurgency in the post–Cold War world. During the 1970s and 1980s, the United States, the Soviet Union, and their proxies regularly supported insurgencies throughout the world. Each shared a belief that toppling or weakening ideologically hostile governments was a strategic necessity, even if the country in question was far from its shores. Moscow, for example, supported leftist insurgents, both directly and indirectly, in Nicaragua, El Salvador, Somalia, Ethiopia, South Africa, and elsewhere, while the United States backed anticommunist groups in Afghanistan, Angola, Nicaragua, Albania, Laos, and Tibet, among other places. However, ideological conflicts such as those in El Salvador, Nicaragua, Afghanistan, and Angola all began to lose significant superpower (and related allied-bloc) support during the latter part of the 1980s. With the collapse of the Soviet Union, the major powers no longer backed or opposed a movement or government based on its profession of Marxist ideology.[19] More significantly, once ideologically driven conflicts such as those in Angola and Afghanistan quickly transformed into religious, tribal, or ethnic entities (or simply removed the veneer of ideology) it became apparent that superpower backing was no longer obtainable simply by claiming to be communist or anticommunist.

Plunder

Supporting insurgencies can also bring material benefits to states, particularly to military personnel or politicians closely linked with the guerrillas. Ugandan military officers, for example, have benefited significantly from the activities of the CRD-ML and the MLC, both of which have raped the Congo of its natural resources on behalf of their sponsor. Uganda has employed the Rassemblement Congolais pour la Democratie to seize a variety of resources, in part to pay for

---

[19]One exception was Guatemala, where guerrillas continued to receive substantial aid from Cuba. However, this ended when a formal peace agreement was signed in 1996.

the cost of the insurgency.[20]   Similarly, the Revolutionary United Front (RUF) in Sierra Leone has shared its largesse with Monrovia, and the Khmer Rouge in Cambodia worked hand-in-glove with corrupt Thai military officers before the group's collapse in the latter half of the 1990s. In the same vein, Pakistani officers and intelligence officials have ties to the Taliban, many of whom have benefited from Afghanistan's shadow export market, as well as the Golden Crescent's cross-border narcotics trade. Although governments seldom initially back insurgencies for financial reasons, subsequent opportunities for enrichment often create a vested interest in continuing support with an important constituency.

As the above review suggests, a plethora of considerations may lead a state to back an insurgency. Nearly every state supporter had multiple reasons for backing a particular rebel group. Often the motivations mentioned worked in concert. Although strategic rationales were among the most important reasons states supported insurgencies, domestic concerns—including a desire to placate key constituents or to crush dissidents—were also common motivations. Sometimes states sought to help embattled coreligionists or ethnic kin, although this assistance was almost always motivated by deeper realpolitik concerns as well. As discussed in Chapter Six, this geopolitical emphasis often makes states difficult or unreliable sources of support for insurgence. This lack of reliability has encouraged rebel movements to seek and exploit other forms of external assistance, as described in the next three chapters.

---

[20]In addition to gold, diamonds, and copper, the Congo's guerrillas also seek columbite-tantalite, a rare mineral used in the manufacture of several sophisticated products (Vick, 2001, p. 1).

Chapter Three

DIASPORA SUPPORT FOR INSURGENCIES

States are neither the only nor necessarily the most important sponsors of insurgent movements. Diasporas—immigrant communities established in other countries—frequently support insurgencies in their homelands.[1] Despite being separated by thousands of miles, homeland struggles are often keenly felt among immigrant communities. Indeed, insurgents in Algeria, Azerbaijan, Egypt, India (Punjab and Kashmir), Indonesia (Aceh), Ireland, Israel, Lebanon, Russia, Rwanda, Sri Lanka, Turkey, Northern Ireland, and Kosovo have all received various and important forms of support from their respective migrant communities.

Significant diaspora support has occurred in every region of the globe, except Latin America.[2] Migrant communities have sent money, arms, and recruits back to their home countries, which have proven pivotal in sustaining insurgent campaigns. This support has at times significantly increased insurgents' capabilities and enabled them to withstand government counterinsurgency efforts.

Reliance on diasporas to wage an insurgency may become an increasingly common phenomenon in years to come. Such fundraising efforts are hardly new: Palestinian movements have done so for decades as have the Kurdish Workers Party (PKK) and the

---

[1] For a review of diaspora politics, see Sheffer (1994); and Anthony Smith (1995), pp. 1–19. For more on the financial contributions of diasporas to homeland conflict, see Collier and Hoeffler (2000); and Shain and Sherman (1998), pp. 321–346.

[2] Latin America's exceptional status may be explained because diaspora support tends to be directed at ethnic insurgencies, which in general are rare in Latin America.

PIRA, which have long relied on Kurds in Germany and Irish-Americans, respectively, to provide needed funds. But diasporas may be more important should state funding stop or become unobtainable, forcing insurgent groups to look elsewhere to sustain their struggle. The withdrawal of superpower support in the early 1990s has already caused the collapse of several insurgencies that depended on Moscow to survive. In addition, the increasing number of ethnic or communal insurgencies relative to ideological conflicts increases the relative prevalence of diaspora support.[3]

This chapter analyzes the scope and dimensions of diaspora support for insurgencies. It provides an in-depth examination of how the LTTE has harnessed its overseas migrant community, using it for funding, arms running, and a host of other activities. The LTTE's experience is not typical, but rather represents the apex of how an insurgent organization can exploit a diaspora for its own ends. Drawing on the LTTE's experience, as well as that of other insurgencies, the chapter then describes the reasons why immigrant communities often support insurgencies in their native lands and examines the difficulties that many host governments have in halting this form of assistance. The chapter concludes with a brief discussion of the utility of diaspora-backing in general and its value relative to states.

THE LTTE AND THE TAMIL DIASPORA

The LTTE is commonly recognized as one of the most sophisticated and deadly insurgencies in the world. The group retains effective control over significant stretches of northeast Sri Lanka, having run a virtual state within a state in the Jaffna peninsula until the Sri Lankan Armed Forces (SLAF) dislodged them in 1995. The LTTE has also repeatedly demonstrated its ability to operate along the entire guerrilla conflict spectrum: from selective assassination, to indiscriminate acts of terrorism, to full-scale, battalion-sized assaults. Colombo has long proven unable to defeat the Tigers militarily. While the dedication of the LTTE's fighters and the SLAF's incompetence are important factors in accounting for the group's

---

[3]For documentation of this shift, see Byman and Van Evera (1998), pp. 39–43.

success, far more critical is the international support infrastructure the LTTE has developed to exploit its diaspora. However, in contrast to the insurgencies in the Congo, the LTTE enjoys strong support among Tamils in Sri Lanka and commands considerable resources. Thus, it requires less outside support and, even if this were cut off, probably would still remain a potent, if diminished, political and military force.

This section provides a brief overview of the essential features of the LTTE international support structure. Its purpose is to demonstrate just how effective diaspora assistance can be when integrated into a global network. The LTTE, as previously noted, is arguably unique. With the possible exception of the PKK and the PIRA, no other group has come close to establishing the type of structure the LTTE has.

The LTTE network straddles the globe and effectively integrates the Tamil diaspora into one overarching external system that constitutes the lifeline for LTTE guerrillas on the ground. This support structure can be subdivided into two main areas: propaganda and finance generation. A third type of support, arms procurement, which does not involve the Tamil diaspora, is discussed in Appendix B. Although each component nominally operates independently of the other, their activities inevitably overlap and are coordinated under the auspices of the group's International Secretariat.[4]

Publicity and Propaganda

The chief architects of LTTE publicity and propaganda are Anton Balasingham and Sivagnam Gopalarathinam, who, together, oversee the group's overseas political activities. Their objective is to galvanize international support for the Tiger cause while discrediting Colombo by disseminating a consistent three-fold message:

- Tamils are the innocent victims of Sinhalese discrimination and government-instigated military repression.

---

[4]Currently run by Velummylum Manoharan and contained within the LTTE Central Governing Committee, this particular body has the responsibility of managing all external support operations and ensuring that they are effectively brought to bear on LTTE guerrilla actions taken on the ground in Sri Lanka. Manoharan replaced Lawrence Thiligar as head of the International Secretariat in early 1997.

- The LTTE represents the only vehicle capable of defending and promoting the interests of the Sri Lankan Tamil community.

- There can be no peace in Sri Lanka until the country's Tamils are granted their own independent state under the governance of the LTTE (Davis, 1996b).

Balasingham and Gopalarathinam head a quasidiplomatic structure that consists of sympathetic pressure groups, media units, charities, and benevolent nongovernmental organizations (NGOs). Although, as of 1998, the Tigers were represented in 54 countries as far-flung as Burma and Botswana, their political activity concentrates on Western states that have large Tamil expatriate communities, including, most notably, the United Kingdom, Canada, Australia, France, and Switzerland.[5] Overarching front organizations have been established to harness and integrate political support. These allegedly include the United Tamil Organization (UTO) in the United Kingdom, the Federation of Associations of Canadian Tamils (FACT) in Canada, the Australasian Federation of Tamil Associations in Australia, the French Federation of Tamil Associations in France, and the Swiss Federation of Tamil Associations in Switzerland.[6]

In addition to front groups, the LTTE has effectively exploited the liberal democratic ethos that underscores many Western states to establish offices that are openly representative of the Tiger cause. Foremost among these is Eelam House in London, which acts as the LTTE's principal headquarters outside Sri Lanka. Although nominally headed by A. C. Shanthan, the LTTE Chief in the United Kingdom, it serves as Balasingham's principal base of operations for coordinating overseas political activity; it is also the location from which all official Tiger statements, memoranda, and proclamations emanate.[7]

---

[5]Personal correspondence with officials of the Sri Lankan High Commission, Ottawa, November 2000. The Ilankai Tamil Sangam USA (The Association of Tamils of Sri Lanka in the United States) disseminates information concerning the conflict in Sri Lanka in the United States that is not favorable to the Sri Lankan government.

[6]See, for instance, Ranetunge (2000).

[7]For an overview of many of the coordinating functions carried out by Eelam House, and its links with other pro-LTTE groups, see *The Island* (2000).

LTTE propaganda targets both the Tamil diaspora and the host government. This aspect of the group's war effort is conducted at an extremely sophisticated level and is far more potent than the countercampaign of the Sri Lankan state. Propaganda is disseminated in a number of ways, including: electronic mail; the Internet; telephone hot lines; community libraries; mailings; Tamil television programs and radio broadcasts; and political, cultural, and social gatherings (Gunaratna, 2000b). These latter events are often coordinated with venerated dates in the LTTE calendar such as Martyrs Day, which is celebrated annually on November 27—Prabhakaran's birthday.[8] Meetings of this sort are generally organized both to maximize mobilization among committed LTTE adherents as well as to sway potentially sympathetic supporters and liberals in the West:

> The celebrations are usually held at a hall, stadium or in an open area. The place is covered with thousands of display material carrying the faces of martyrs and their names. . . . The converted Tamils who believe in having their separate state. . .come to venerate these martyrs. . . . Generally, the chief guest at these functions is a Westerner. He initiates the ceremony and delivers a speech supporting the struggle of Tamils in Sri Lanka. The speech is followed by other Westerners who [are prepared to help] spread the Tiger message in various lobby groups. After the speeches the hall is enveloped in darkness while search lights flash and the sound of the battlefield rocks the crowd. The main screen carries the portrait of a martyr and how he paid with his life to give vigor to the struggle. . . . Then a group of young women [will enter] on stage and dance to martial music and stories of heroism. . . . Lastly, the younger generation [will] stage their act requesting a Tiger uncle to come and save the Tamils. (*Terrorist Group Celebrates Martyrs Day in Australia,* 2000.)

The LTTE is especially reliant on electronic propaganda disseminated via the World Wide Web, news groups (Usenet), and email. The LTTE has established a prominent presence on the Internet, with many of its web sites fully documented and indexed in popular search engines.[9] A number of them contain links and other jump-off

---

[8]Personal correspondence with officials of the Sri Lankan High Commission, Canberra, December 2000.

[9]As of July 2001, leading pro-LTTE web sites included: www.eelam.com—largely suspected of being the official LTTE web site; www.eelamweb.com—publicly declared

points that are networked—under the banner of "peace"—to internationally renowned humanitarian and development agencies such as the World Council of Churches, the International Educational Development Inc., and the Robert Kennedy Memorial Center for Human Rights. These web sites have enabled the LTTE to establish a truly global presence, permitting the group to "virtually" and instantaneously transmit propaganda, mobilize active supporters, and sway potential backers. This facet has been effectively brought to bear both in "Tamil-rich" states as well as other countries where the group does not have a substantial or well-established ethnic presence, such as the United States and New Zealand.

Most commentators concur that the LTTE is far ahead of the Sri Lankan government in the propaganda war. This shortcoming has allowed the group to continually embarrass Colombo and gain political capital at its expense.[10] Although the government is now beginning to appreciate the critical role of positive publicity in prosecuting the war against the LTTE—reflected by the appointment of information counselors in many of the country's overseas missions—the overall sophistication of its approach remains far from adequate and much less so than the pro-Tiger lobby. As insurgency analyst Sisira Pinnawala (1998) observes with respect to propaganda heightening and dampening activities that take place on the Internet:

> The major distinction between the pro-Tamil struggle Websites and those belonging to the other camp is operational sophistication. Pro-Tamil Websites cater to a wider audience, [providing] a full service [that caters to the] cultural and social needs of the Tamil community. . . . There has also been [a vigorous] attempt. . .to introduce multimedia, including real-time video. . . . The government approach on the Internet is totally the opposite of the above. It is characterized by old Soviet style propaganda. . . . None of the government-operated Websites have attempted to attract audiences

---

Eelam supporter with a multimedia content; www.tamilcanadian.com—openly supports the Eelam cause but is more moderate than the above two sites, directing its message to a wider Tamil audience; www.tamilnet.com—openly supports the creation of an independent Tamil state of Eelam, but attempts to do so a non-partisan reporter; and www.tamilforum.com—supports the creation of an independent Eelam state and is an apologist for the LTTE.

[10]Personal correspondence with Sri Lankan officials and commentators, Ottawa, London, and Bangkok, November–December 2000.

from among the Sri Lankans overseas by addressing their needs. . .like the pro-LTTE camp. There is, in other words, no full service approach.

The effectiveness of the LTTE propaganda campaign can be gauged by the high degree of legitimacy the group has among many Western states, which is the main focus of Tiger international publicity activities. For most of the 1990s, the LTTE was portrayed as a genuine national liberation movement engaged in a legitimate struggle for independence against an oppressive Sinhalese-dominated state. In common with such internationally respected entities as the ANC and the PLO, the group has been permitted to establish representative offices, dispatch political "counselors," and engage in unrestricted and open-ended lobbying activities. This political success occurs despite the LTTE's involvement in numerous terrorist atrocities and human rights violations during the decade, including:

- The assassinations of Indian and Sri Lankan presidents in 1991 and 1993;

- The 1992 massacre of 166 Muslims in Palliyagodella;

- The 1995 massacre of 42 Sinhalese villagers at Kallarawa, near Trincomalee;

- Several suicide attacks in and near Colombo from 1995–1998 that left hundreds dead and thousands injured. The 1996 bombing of the Central Branch killed 90 and injured over 1,400 others widely recognized to be one of the most devastating terrorist attacks ever;

- The attempted assassination of the current Sri Lankan president, Chandrika Bandaranaike Kumaratunga, in December 1999;

- The regular assassinations of leading Tamil moderates and scholars;

- The assassinations of the Minister of Industrial Development and Deputy Mayor of Mount Lavinia in June 2000;[11]

---

[11]*LTTE Atrocities*, internal document supplied to author, December 2000. See also Manoi Joshi (1996), pp. 29–31; *The Courier Mail* (1996); *The Australian* (1996); *The Courier Mail* (1997); *The Australian* (1997).

- The recurrent use of children as frontline combatants.[12]

Certain governments have begun to take a harder line against the LTTE in recent years. In 1997, the group was included on the newly promulgated U.S. list of foreign terrorist organizations (FTOs), a designation that makes it illegal to belong to the LTTE, raise funds for it, or openly support its aims in the United States. The State Department has since declared FACT as well as the World Tamil Movement (WTM) and World Tamil Association, as Tiger fronts and subject to the same provisions (Ranetunge, 2000, p. 3; *The National Post,* 2000d; *The Bangkok Post,* 1997; *Washington Post,* 1999; *Daily News,* 1999).

In 1999, Ottawa also declared the LTTE a terrorist organization and affirmed that it would review possible measures that could be instituted to limit the group's activities in Canada (see Kelly and Bryden 1999, pp. 23–39; *The Hindustan Times,* 1998). As with Washington, several other bodies have subsequently been designated fronts for the group, including the WTM (Toronto and Montreal); FACT; the Tamil Coordinating Committee; the Eelam Tamil Associations of Canada, Quebec, and British Columbia; and the Tamil Rehabilitation Organization (see *The National Post,* 2000e).

Most recently, in February 2001, the United Kingdom introduced statutory provisions aimed at preventing extremists from using Britain as a base from which to plan and commit terrorist acts in third countries.[13] The LTTE was among the outlawed groups.

The practical effect of these initiatives should not be overstated, however. Canada has yet to enact any specific legislation against the LTTE or other proscribed fronts, many of which still receive federal, provincial, and local grants for their community and charitable activities. Both intelligence and law enforcement officials agree that

---

[12]See Machel (1977). See also Gunaratna (1998a), p. 2; Goodwin-Gill and Cohn (1994), p. 31; and *The Globe and Mail* (1998a). Sri Lanka's Directorate of Military Intelligence estimates that as many as 60 percent of LTTE cadres are under the age of 18. Even if that figure is exaggerated, concerted assessments of LTTE fighters killed in action reveal that at least 40 percent are between the ages of 9 and 18.

[13]*The Economist* (2001), p. 38. See also *The Economist* (2000g); and *The Deccan Herald* (2000). The proposed legislation will, in effect, represent an extension of the provisions of the 1989 Prevention of Terrorism Act to areas and groups beyond Northern Ireland.

there is little prospect of restrictive measures being introduced in the short-to-medium term.[14] The U.S. statutory provisions do not prevent the Tigers from working through sympathetic cultural and social Tamil NGOs, something that will certainly hold for the United Kingdom's antiterrorism legislation.[15]

It is also important to remember that, in many respects, the changing attitudes of the United States, Canada, and the United Kingdom represent the exception rather than the rule. There are numerous countries where the LTTE continues to enjoy varying degrees of legitimacy and tolerance and, as such, remains free to conduct propaganda and fundraising in a largely unimpeded manner. The countries include South Africa, Norway, Sweden, Switzerland, France, Germany, New Zealand, and Australia.

Fundraising

Alongside propaganda, the LTTE runs a sophisticated international revenue-generating operation that draws heavily on diaspora contributions. There are four main important contributions: direct contributions from migrant communities; funds siphoned off contributions given to NGOs, charities, and benevolent donor groups; people-smuggling; and investments made in legitimate, Tamil-run businesses.[16] The exact amount or percentage breakdown drawn from each of these sources is not known. Combined, however, they

---

[14]Personal correspondence with Canadian Security Intelligence Service officials, Ottawa, November 2000. See also *The National Post* (2000e).

[15]It should also be noted that despite designating the LTTE as an FTO, the United States has yet to take any specific action against the group. According to one informed source, the extent of attrition activities currently taking place in the country are little more than regular monitoring and surveillance conducted by the Federal Bureau of Investigation. Email correspondence with South Asian security and terrorism specialist, January 2001. Personal correspondence with officials of the UK Ministry of Defence, London, December 2000; discussion with senior Department of State counterterrorism official, November 2000.

[16]The LTTE is also alleged to raise money through drug trafficking, running heroin from the Golden Crescent, through India and Sri Lanka, to the West. It should be noted, however, that definitive proof linking the Tigers to an official policy of narcotics trafficking has yet to emerge.

are thought to provide at least $50 million a year in operating revenue.[17]

A significant amount of the money used to support the LTTE insurgency is raised from the international Tamil diaspora. The LTTE focuses on countries that have large Tamil expatriate communities, particularly the United Kingdom, Canada, and Australia.[18] Combined, these three countries are conservatively estimated to provide up to $1.5 million a month to the LTTE cause (see, for instance, Davis, 1996b, p. 35; *Daily News*, 1998; *International Herald Tribune*, 1998; and *Lanka Outlook*, 1998a, pp. 24–25). Most of this money is procured via a standard, baseline "tax" that is imposed, as a minimum obligation, on all families living in the respective host state. In Canada, the 1999 sum ran to $240 a year per household (the equivalent of one Canadian dollar per day); according to informed sources, the group now expects $646 a year from all individuals who are employed.[19]

The Tigers prefer to procure this money voluntarily, relying on the effectiveness of positive publicity to galvanize contributors. When their solicitations fail to procure donations voluntarily, however, the Tigers quickly resort to intimidation and coercion: threatening family members who may remain in LTTE-controlled areas in Sri Lanka or threatening the unwilling contributors themselves.

The scale of contributions derived from the diaspora community is intrinsically related to LTTE effectiveness on the battlefield. Follow-

---

[17]Personal correspondence with South Asian security and terrorism specialist, Hawaii, August 2000. This figure also includes estimates of revenue from narcotics trafficking. See also *The National Post* (2000b); and *Times of India* (2000).

[18]Despite this focus, communities in countries that have smaller numbers of immigrants, such as Norway and Switzerland, have often contributed disproportionately to the LTTE's war chest.

[19]Gunaratna (2000b), p. 74. A figure of 300 UK pounds annually per family has also been quoted by Gunaratna for UK diaspora contributions. See *SBS Dateline* (2000). To facilitate the procurement of diaspora contributions, the LTTE makes use of a database that contains the names and addresses of expatriate Tamils living in important Western communities such as Canada, Australia, and the United Kingdom. A variety of information is stored on the system, including statistics pertaining to education qualifications, special skills, professions, political affiliations, employment, income level. and the amount of money sent to relatives and family members in Sri Lanka. See Gunaratna (2000b), pp. 75–76; and *The National Post* (2000c).

ing setbacks and defeats, donations typically fall and may have to be coerced from the migrant community. In the wake of major military victories, however, there is likely to be a surge of voluntary, even enthusiastic, financial support, including the proffering of mass spontaneous contributions far in excess of the expected minimum war tax. After the Tigers' widely published capture of Elephant Pass in 2000, for example,[20] there were reports throughout Canada, Australia, and the United Kingdom of a major infusion of donations.[21] According to officials with the Sri Lankan High Commission in Canberra, there were also numerous instances of spontaneous contributions, including on-the-spot pledges of watches, rings, bracelets, and other forms of jewelry.[22]

In the United States, financial contributions are procured more from a small number of wealthy individuals than the expatriate community at large. A leading benefactor is Shan Sunder, a prominent medical practitioner living in California who has made no secret of his support for the creation of an independent Tamil Eelam. He is believed to be one of the most important contributors to the LTTE cause, offering an estimated $4 million over the last decade.

Funds are not always directly procured from the diaspora community. Often the LTTE will siphon off contributions given to nonprofit NGOs, benevolent donor bodies, and other front organizations that finance Tamil social service, development, and rehabilitation programs in Sri Lanka. In these cases, it is particularly difficult to prove that funds raised for humanitarian purposes are being diverted to propagate terrorism or other forms of illegal activity elsewhere.[23] This is particularly true in countries such as Norway, where there is

---

[20]The capture of Elephant Pass was seen as a major victory for the LTTE as it heralded the group's possible recapture of the Jaffna Peninsula. See *The Economist* (2000b,c); and *CNN Interactive Worldwide News* (2000a,b,c).

[21]Personal correspondence with officials of the Canadian Security Intelligence Service and Sri Lankan High Commission, Ottawa, November 2000.

[22]It has been tentatively suggested that in the immediate aftermath of Elephant Pass's fall, overall contributions to the Tigers may have increased by as much as three times. In the absence of definitive data, however, such estimates are difficult to confidently endorse. Personal correspondence between Sri Lankan officials, Ottawa and Canberra, November-December 2000.

[23]Personal correspondence between UK defense and Australian intelligence officials, London and Canberra, December 2000.

no a legal requirement to register an organization before engaging in fundraising (see *Lanka Outlook*, 1998a, p. 24). As noted above, this is one of the main problems currently confronting those states that have sought to introduce legislation aimed at constraining the financial activities of proscribed groups on their soil.

The LTTE is also thought to raise money through organized people-smuggling, which is now believed to constitute a mainstay of Tiger financial procurement. According to intelligence officials in Canada, Australia, and the United Kingdom, the group is playing a pivotal role in smuggling illegal migrants and refugees out of Sri Lanka and India to the West, charging between \$18,000 and \$32,000 per transaction.[24] The overall scope of this trade is difficult to determine. However, in June 2000, the Sri Lankan Criminal Investigation Department (CID) uncovered one major LTTE smuggling ring, involving an estimated 600 to 700 people who had been trafficked to the European Union on forged visas (see *Daily News*, 2000; and *Daily Mirror*, 2000). After taking overhead costs into account, the net profits from such an operation would still have been substantial, running into millions of dollars.

The Tigers allegedly make considerable use of Thailand for human trafficking—both as an identification forgery hub as well as a staging point for onward journeys. The group is thought to have established a small but effective cadre of intermediaries in Bangkok who facilitate the physical movement of migrants across national borders. Such a modus operandi is also seen as a way of distancing senior LTTE members from possible prosecution in the event a smuggling ring is broken up or otherwise penetrated by law enforcement authorities.[25]

Canada is the destination of choice for the bulk of the LTTE's human cargo, both on account of its large Tamil diaspora (which facilitates rapid local integration into the adopted society) and the extremely

---

[24]Personal interviews between defense and intelligence officials, London, Ottawa, Bangkok, and Canberra, November–December 2000.

[25]Personal correspondence with Sri Lankan High Commission officials, Bangkok, December 2000.

weak immigration laws currently put into effect by Ottawa.[26] Once they are in the country, the migrants quickly go underground and generally take low-paying menial jobs that have been prearranged by the LTTE. This ensures that the new arrivals remain semipermanently indentured to the group. In current Sri Lankan context, this translates to acting as local Tiger henchmen and/or debt collectors.[27]

A final diaspora-related source for LTTE funding comes from investments in legitimate business and commercial holdings. In many cases, these enterprises run on a system of ownership by proxy, where the Tigers cover initial capital costs and then split the subsequent profits with the company's ostensible owner. The LTTE has established a number of businesses ventures that work in this manner. The most prominent include the gold and jewelry trade, wholesale commodity freight and distribution, and the provision of local Tamil computer, telephone, and bus services. Because of a lack of reliable data, it is not possible to provide a definitive figure for the amount of money the LTTE generates from these sources. However, according to Rohan Gunaratna, a specialist on the LTTE at the Centre for the Study of Terrorism and Political Violence at the University of St. Andrews, Scotland, the revenue earned from Canada—the main locus for this form of financial procurement—can be roughly estimated at $6.5 million for the period between October 1998 and October 1999 (2000b, pp. 77–82; *The National Post,* 2000c).

These global financial operations have enabled the LTTE to mount protracted and expensive legal defenses for the group and its mem-

---

[26]Police and intelligence officials believe that the LTTE-Canadian smuggling route operates according to a basic procedure. Clients first travel to Bangkok, often on stolen passports that have been doctored for the purpose, where they await the provision of forged identity documents such as passports, driver licenses, and residency cards. Onward journeys to Canada are then arranged. Direct routes are avoided because the chances of interdiction at major airports such as Toronto, Montreal, and Vancouver tend to be too great. Migrants therefore are smuggled through U.S. points of entry where, so long as their papers are correctly crafted, they will not be required to present an incoming visa. It is then just a matter of crossing over one of the many land borders between the two countries, the majority of which perform only perfunctory and largely superficial immigrant checks. Personal correspondence with Sri Lankan intelligence officials, Bangkok, December 2000. See also Charu Joshi (2000) and *National Post* (2000a).

[27]Personal correspondence with Canadian and Sri Lankan intelligence officials, Ottawa and Bangkok, November–December 2000.

bers. This has been best reflected by the example of Manikavaagam Suresh, the LTTE's chief representative in Canada. Declared a threat to national security in 1995 and served with a deportation order in 1997, Suresh has yet to be sent back to Sri Lanka. He has been released from prison and remains free to move around his home city of Toronto in a largely unrestricted fashion.[28]

Funds raised from overseas also form an integral component of the group's so-called National Defense Fund and general weapons procurement efforts.[29] The importance of this external support should not be underestimated. Indeed, since the LTTE lost control of the Jaffna Peninsula in 1995, it is believed that as much as 90 to 95 percent of the LTTE war budget comes from overseas.[30] There is little doubt that without this economic backing, the group's ability to continue with the Tamil Eelam struggle would be significantly reduced.

Conclusion

The LTTE insurgency and its diaspora are intimately tied to one another. So long as the group can use its diaspora to raise funds, its guerrilla and terrorist campaign can be sustained. The structure has provided most, if not all, of the ingredients required for any successful insurgency—from international legitimization and recognition to money, munitions, and access to secure external logistical bases. This will probably further entrench the noncompromising attitude of the Tiger leadership and, in so doing, block any meaningful progress toward a negotiated settlement based on political compromise.

---

[28]Personal correspondence with officials of the Canadian Security Intelligence Service, Ottawa, November 2000. See also *The National Post* (2000c); *The Island* (1998); and *The National Post* (1999). While the lack of judicial precedent (in terms of deporting a recognized refugee for reasons of national security) is one factor that has worked in Suresh's favor, another is the high-powered legal counsel assembled on his behalf. This defense team has mounted a series of successful appeals against the 1997 deportation, bringing the case before the Supreme Court and ensuring it as one of the most keenly contested in Canadian legal history.

[29]For an overview of the LTTE's global arms procurement efforts, see Chalk (2000b).

[30]Personal correspondence with Sri Lankan intelligence and government officials, Colombo, May 1999.

By permitting the LTTE to open offices and establish representation, Western countries have unwittingly blessed the group's political and military agenda. LTTE propaganda and fundraising activities conducted in Europe, Australasia, and North America have proved pivotal to its ongoing terrorist and guerrilla campaign in Sri Lanka. Moreover, the generally unrestrained liberal democratic freedom that the LTTE enjoys in these states has enabled the group to slowly build and develop a complex, multilayered, and truly integrated global support structure that has become difficult to detect and root out.

MOTIVATIONS FOR DIASPORA SUPPORT

Diaspora motivations differ considerably from those of state sponsors. As noted in Chapter Two, governments back insurgencies primarily for strategic reasons; seldom is support for ethnic or religious brethren enough to prompt a regime to back a rebel movement. Migrant communities, in contrast, are motivated largely by a desire to support a kinship group.[31] Indeed, almost inherent to the idea of a diaspora is a concept of homeland. Communities abroad often feel a genuine sympathy for the domestic struggles of their overseas kin. Sometimes these communities may also feel a sense of guilt because they are safe while their kin are involved in a brutal and bloody struggle. Insurgent groups play on this sympathy and guilt to gain financial and political support.

Insurgent efforts to raise money from diasporas often enjoy a bandwagon effect. Military victories tend to capture greater support from abroad, which in turn provides more money for continued success in the domestic theater. The LTTE, for instance, enjoyed a major boost in its overseas fundraising efforts following the group's capture of Elephant Pass in 2000. When groups fail to perform on the battlefield, however, support can quickly dry up as immigrants begin to view the guerrilla campaign as a lost cause.

---

[31]The reality of kinship ties may be limited, but the perception is often quite strong. The perception of a shared homeland can be based on those of common ancestry, language, historical experience, or other ascriptive factors.

Diasporas may sometimes contribute to an insurgency for ideological as well as communal reasons. Some Tamils, for example, share the LTTE's vague Marxist ideals as well as its vision of Tamil independence. This was also the case with many Palestinians who backed leftist organizations, such as the Popular Front for the Liberation of Palestine, the Democratic Front for the Liberation of Palestine, and the Popular Front for the Liberation of Palestine–General Command. In general, however, an insurgency's ideological bent is far less important to diaspora communities than its representation of a particular community's political and military aspirations.

Sometimes immigrants support insurgents as a result of coercion by the movement's overseas representatives.[32] Diaspora communities are often tightly bound and isolated with as much of their commerce, policing, and other basic functions being handled within the community as possible.[33] If insurgents can influence the politics of these self-contained units, they may be able to force immigrant workers to contribute a share of their wages to the group and coerce businessmen to make donations to the cause. Often, the insurgents' pressure is indirect. Tamil representatives seeking to raise money for the LTTE struggle, for example, emphasize the general importance of the cause and the need for their community to stand by the guerrillas. Should voluntary support prove insufficient, however, threats to relatives in the homeland or to the business or lives of the immigrants are likely to follow. Involuntary backing of this sort is likely if the insurgents are also involved in informal community policing. The PKK provides a good example of this. Thanks to its penetration of European Kurdish communities, the PKK has been able to exert considerable pressure on diaspora members to donate funds.[34]

---

[32]Individuals who contribute because of coercion can hardly be called supporters. In many cases, such as with the Tamil diaspora, the threat of coercion and genuine sympathy for the cause often work hand-in-hand.

[33]For a review of this "in group" policing and mentality in general, see Fearon and Laitin (1996), pp. 715–735.

[34]Gunaratna (1999), pp. 351–355.

WHY HOST GOVERNMENTS DO NOT BLOCK DIASPORA SUPPORT

As the LTTE's experience makes clear, the key to constricting diaspora support is not found in conflict-ravaged homelands but in the cities and along the borders of states with numerous immigrants who underwrite the insurgency. Several problems, however, hinder efforts to restrict, much less prohibit, diaspora support. These problems are particularly acute in the United States and other liberal democracies that enjoy broad and protected civil liberties.

Host governments often have difficulty differentiating between non-insurgent immigrants and pro-insurgent activists; to the benefit of the LTTE, Western governments and law enforcement agencies have found it difficult to differentiate between law-abiding Tamils and pro-LTTE activists. Gaining this knowledge requires intelligence and law enforcement agencies to actively monitor immigrant communities, a decision that is inherently costly, controversial, and anathema to the ethos of Western democracies.

In addition, the insurgents may exercise more political clout in their immigrant diaspora than the government trying to counter it. This is particularly true in the West, where politicians tend to be sympathetic to the political aspirations and the grievances of minority groups in their constituencies. Many politicians running for office in Toronto, Montreal, and Vancouver, for example, believe the ethnic Tamil vote can tip the electoral balance in their favor. The Sinhalese-dominated Sri Lankan government enjoys no similar ability to concentrate the minds of Canadian politicians.

An insurgency's propaganda campaign matters immensely in these circumstances. Because the Tigers have run such an effective publicity campaign, and Colombo's own effort has long been so feeble, Western politicians are often reluctant or averse to supporting tough actions against the LTTE and its activities among its diaspora. Radical Islamist groups, by contrast, have found little support among Western politicians (even though several Western countries have large and devout Muslim communities) because they are widely seen as violent, irrational, and anti-Western.

Equally important, the diaspora often tends to place few, if any, demands on host governments, while their state opponents are often seen as interfering or pressuring. Viewed from another perspective, if governments do nothing, they tacitly accede to the wishes of the insurgents, who are then free to organize and fundraise. The government opposing the insurgency, in contrast, must press for the host government to enforce border and export controls, gather intelligence, restrict fundraising, and otherwise take several difficult and intrusive steps to shut down the diaspora's activities in that country. In addition, the embattled government is also asking the host state to expand resources in a way that provides no obvious or direct benefit.

Sometimes governments may not be able to exercise sufficient control in order to curtail a diaspora's activities on behalf of an insurgent group. The LTTE, for instance, has exploited lax law enforcement, rampant corruption, and inefficient border security in Thailand to establish highly effective logistical hubs for the movement of weapons and people. As one intelligence official remarked, whereas the West forms the financial heart of the Tigers, Thailand constitutes the essential lifeline for the group's war effort in Sri Lanka. Without the critical logistical infrastructure that has been established in Thailand to import and export weapons, the organization would not be able to thrive as it does.[35] Thailand, like many Western countries, is not eager to take on the difficult task of reigning in the LTTE. However, in contrast to governments in Europe and the United States, it would be questionable whether the Thai government has the ability, much less the will, to do so.

The host government's ability to affect the insurgency, however, goes beyond legal measures designed to constrict support networks. The strength and longevity of diaspora assistance also depends heavily

---

[35]Personal correspondence with Sri Lankan intelligence official, Bangkok, December 2000. Bangkok has long dismissed claims, for lack of evidence, that the LTTE exploits its territory for the movement of arms. In April 2000, however, the government was forced to concede that weapons movements were, in fact, taking place in the country, following the accidental discovery of a Tiger logistics cell on the resort island of Phuket. The base, which has since been identified as part of a wider network embracing Ranong, Krabi, Sattahip, and Songkla, led to revelations that Prime Minister Chuan Leekpai had specifically ordered military intelligence to hush LTTE arms trafficking activities taking place in the southern part of the country. According to one well-placed individual in the army, the gag order had been issued for fear that widespread publicity would generate increased pressure on Bangkok to adopt a more concerted line against the Tigers and that this would, in turn, provoke retaliatory actions directly on Thai soil. See *The Bangkok Post* (2000a,b).

on the attitude and activities of its host nation. Two particularly important policies to measure are the host government's willingness to actively police immigrant communities and that society's willingness to assimilate immigrants. If insurgents' control over migrant communities can be curtailed, involuntary support is likely to decrease. Further, if diasporas are allowed to assimilate fully into their adopted countries, links with the homeland and associated identification with the objectives of insurgents operating there are likely to diminish too.

Not surprisingly, many insurgent movements actively try to hinder and prevent assimilation and otherwise prevent the host state from weakening the community's emotional ties to their homeland. The PKK, both in Germany and elsewhere in Europe, for example, has struggled hard to prevent Kurdish assimilation as has the LTTE with respect to Tamils living in the United Kingdom, Canada, Switzerland, Norway, and Australia.

THE LIMITED RANGE OF DIASPORA SUPPORT

Diaspora support at times plays a critical role in helping groups sustain themselves financially, but it does not offer the same broad range of benefits as state support (e.g., safe havens, military training, sophisticated weapons, diplomatic backing, etc.). Financial assistance is by far the most common form of support that migrants provide to insurgent movements. Money, in contrast to material support, crosses borders with ease. Moreover, diasporas often are quite wealthy relative to their homeland brethren, making them ideal sources of funds.

Certain migrant communities may also provide several of other types of support though this occurs rarely. Armenian, Kurdish, and Tamil diasporas have, for example, generated political pressure on their various host governments to help insurgents in Turkey and Sri Lanka or to otherwise oppose the governments they are fighting. In some instances, arms sales even in allied countries were effectively blocked. Members of the Tamil diaspora have additionally championed the Tamil Tiger cause abroad—acting as de facto political representatives of the LTTE—while skilled individuals, such as computer programmers and demolition experts, have assisted with the group's military and fundraising efforts. Hezbollah has also used the

Lebanese Shi'a diaspora to gather intelligence abroad, including information that has aided the group in conducting terrorist attacks on Israeli targets overseas. Summarizing these various activities, Gabriel Sheffer (1994, pp. 64–65) has observed:

> Diasporas [may] engage in a myriad of [pursuits], which may affect the security of those regarded as opponents. [In particular, such communities can be used] to support irredentist, secessionist or national liberation movements. [These] trans-state networks can be used to transfer. . .resources such as fighters, weapons, military intelligence and money. [Such uses make it an] easier task in launching major. . .attacks in their host countries.

A final important note pertains to the various Kashmiri groups and reflects the value of state versus diaspora assistance. The pro-independence JKLF enjoyed substantial backing from many Kashmiris living abroad. However, the group quickly lost ground to the more militant Islamist groups backed by Pakistan even though these organizations appeared to have less popular support among overseas Kashmiris. The arms, haven, training, funding, and other forms of aid Pakistan provided have made the Islamist groups politically and militarily stronger, enabling them to overcome their secular and less pro-Pakistan rivals.

Chapter Four

REFUGEE SUPPORT FOR INSURGENCIES

Refugee flows and insurgencies often feed one another: The discrimination, violence, and misery that typically accompany civil wars often displace populations that in turn contribute to and sustain the original conflict.[1] This phenomenon was common during the Cold War. For example, Soviet brutality in Afghanistan led to the exodus of millions of Afghans, who subsequently became a major impetus behind the anti-Soviet resistance. The problem of refugee flows has recently become even more acute. Table 4.1 compares the total number of refugees in various years over the last two decades. As the totals in the table suggest, the refugee burden was higher for much of the 1990s compared with the decade before the end of the Cold War.

Refugees have played a pivotal role in many insurgencies. The Taliban was formed primarily among displaced Afghans, particularly those who had enrolled as Pakistani seminary students. Indeed, almost every Afghan movement drew upon refugees living in Pakistan, Iran, or other neighboring states. Karen refugees helped sustain the Karen National Union's resistance to the Burmese government, while Palestinian refugees supported the PLO for decades prior to the Oslo Agreement. Hutus and Tutsis who fled Rwanda and Burundi contributed to the continuation of conflict in these countries and, after war spread to the Congo, refugees from the fighting there often joined insurgent movements. Insurgent movements in countries as diverse as Ethiopia, Iraq, the Republic of the Congo,

---

[1]Weiner (1996), pp. 5–42. For a broader review, see Weiner (1993).

Table 4.1

Total Number of Refugees

Year	Number of Refugees
1982	9,800,000
1986	11,600,000
1990	17,190,430
1994	14,488,740
1998	11,491,710

SOURCES: http://www.unhcr.ch/statist/98 oview/tab1_4.htm; United Nations High Commissioner for Refugees, *The State of the World's Refugees: In Search of Solutions* (New York: Oxford University Press, 1995).

NOTE: The figures for the years 1982 and 1986 are rounded.

Russia, Sri Lanka, Sudan, and Tajikistan have in the same manner successfully recruited among refugees. Without such support, these insurgencies would have lacked fighters, money, and a solid organizational base.

This chapter explores how refugees can create and sustain an insurgency, using the experience of the Taliban in Afghanistan to illustrate the impact that refugees have on a successful rebel movement. As with the LTTE experience described in Chapter Three, the Taliban's history is not typical: Rather, it demonstrates how—when the conditions are right—refugees can initiate and prosecute a formidable insurgency and lead it to victory. This chapter concludes by drawing on the Taliban's experience—as well as those of other movements that have relied heavily on refugees—to present more-general lessons, both about refugees' contributions to conflict and about what potential limits restrain their role.

THE TALIBAN AND AFGHANISTAN'S REFUGEES

The Taliban of Afghanistan, the dominant Afghani insurgent movement that today controls over 90 percent of the country, was created and sustained by Afghan refugees living in Pakistan. The Taliban has its roots in the Afghan jihad fought against the Soviet Union in the

1980s. During that time, Afghan guerrilla groups used refugee camps as a place to organize, train, and recruit. Afghan women and children took shelter in Pakistan and Iran, while men fought the Soviets, and at times one another.[2] Devastated by years of war, scores of displaced Afghan youth found their only source of education and upbringing in the puritanical Islamic *madrassas* (seminaries) that sprang up along the Pakistani border. Imbued with an eccentric and virulently discriminatory interpretation of Sunni Islam, these student refugees emerged to form the Taliban militia in the wake of the civil war that was unleashed by the collapse of the mujahedin Afghan government in 1992. The Taliban and its refugee cohorts set out to reunite Afghanistan, bring peace, disarm the population, and establish order under a strict version of the *shari'a* (Islamic law). The movement's leaders absorbed lessons from the Pakistani madrassas, which emphasized the indivisibility of the Islamic community and the need to extend it through force of arms, and soon became a major sponsor of international Islamic movements.

The Taliban appear to enjoy considerable support among many Afghans. These Afghans, even those who do not share the Taliban's extreme religious views, are exhausted by war and welcome any hope of peace. Support is particularly strong among ethnic Pashtuns. Because of this, the Taliban required only limited assistance from outsiders. If Pakistani support had not been provided initially, the group would have found it difficult to gain a critical mass and score initial victories in Afghanistan; over time, however, this support became less important as the Taliban's own skills and resources increased.

Drawing on large numbers of volunteers from Pakistani refugee camps, the Taliban steadily overwhelmed other Afghan factions. The group quickly captured and pacified large tracts of the Afghan countryside, earning widespread respect from the Pashtun population exhausted by war and banditry. This grassroots support proved to be a crucial factor in helping to solidify the internal identity and legitimacy of the Taliban and was certainly a key determinant in the group's capture of Qandahar in 1994 and Kabul in 1996. With the seizure of Mazar-i Sharif on August 8, 1998, the Taliban consolidated

---

[2]For a review, see Urban (1990); and Cordovez and Harrison (1995).

its hold over most, though not all of, Afghanistan, driving the NA,[3] which still holds the country's seat at the United Nations, into a thin sliver of land in the northeast (see Saikal, 1998, pp. 118–119; Khalizad et al., 1999, p. 9; Howard, 2000, p. 28; Rubin, 1999, pp. 79–87; Davis and Rashid, 1998, pp. 43–89).

While the main focus of Taliban insurgent activity since 1994 has been directed toward seizing national power in Afghanistan, the group has also tended to define and pursue wider regional objectives. This has been apparent not only with regard to Central Asia but also to Iran, China (Xinjiang), and Russia (the north Caucasus). Uzbek authorities have long asserted that fundamentalist Islamic revivalism in the Ferghana Valley is directly connected to a deliberate policy of destabilization—orchestrated by the Taliban—and that the Taliban is an important sponsor of the underground Islamic Movement of Uzbekistan (IMU).[4] Officials also believe the Afghan group plays an important role in coordinating the activities of Uzbek, Tajik, and Kyrgyz extremists, using money it derives from heroin trade and from the largesse it receives from wealthy non-Afghan Muslims, such as Usama bin Laden, to help fund an international Islamic training camp in the border regions of northern Afghanistan (Howard, 2000, pp. 34–36; Rashid, 1999, pp. 29–30; *The Far Eastern Economic Review*, 1999; Frantz, 2000; *New York Times*, 2000; *The Economist*, 2000d).

The Afghan refugees were not alone in their campaign to gain control of Afghanistan. The Taliban movement, which coalesced around the leadership of Muhammad Umar in 1994, drew on the military backing of Pakistan and financial support of Saudi Arabia. Most of Islamabad's military assistance backing was channeled through the Jamiat-ul-Ulema-e-Islam (JUI), a radical Islamist political party with strong ties to that country's army, Interior Ministry, and Inter-

---

[3]The NA, which is officially known as the National Islamic United Front for the Salvation of Afghanistan, was formed in 1996. It continues to be recognized as the legitimate government in Afghanistan by all but three states: Pakistan, Saudi Arabia and the United Arab Emirates. The most prominent components of the NA have included the National Islamic Movement of Afghanistan, the Islamic Unity Party of Afghanistan, the Islamic Movement of Afghanistan, the Islamic Party of Afghanistan, and the Council of the East.

[4]Howard (2000), pp. 31–32; Rashid (1999), pp. 28–30; *The Economist* (2000f); *The Far Eastern Economic Review* (1999). The IMU was added to the U.S. State Department's list of FTOs in September 2000.

Services Intelligence (ISI) Department. Between 1994 and 1999, the JUI acted as the Taliban's main recruiter and trainer in Pakistan, drawing primarily upon refugees based in the country's northwest frontier region. This support was in addition to, and quite separate from, the weapons consignments dispatched to Afghanistan as part of Pakistan's publicly stated support for the Taliban.

Pakistan also contributed directly to the Taliban's military campaign with its own forces. Pakistani soldiers have periodically fought in Afghanistan at Islamabad's behest, and Northern Alliance officials claim that Pakistan has at times provided air cover. Pakistan helps the Taliban not only to consolidate its power but also to give Pakistani military forces experience at fighting in difficult terrain under varying conditions—experience that would be useful should a conflict occur with India.

Financial support to the Taliban primarily comes from Saudi Arabia. Although Riyadh directly provided assistance in the mid-1990s, the movement's protection of bin Laden eventually led to the curtailment of all monetary assistance in 1998 (though not of diplomatic recognition). Since then, funds have emanated mainly from wealthy Saudi individuals and members of the clergy, the bulk of which have gone to supporting the Pakistani madrassas, which continue to act as the main recruiting grounds and doctrinal centers for the ongoing Taliban Afghan jihad.[5]

REFUGEE MOTIVATIONS

Refugees generally are motivated by a powerful desire to regain their homeland or to restore their nation's influence over a particular territory. The Soviet invasion of Afghanistan inspired a nationalist, as well as an Islamist, surge as many Afghans took up arms to expel the infidel foreigner. Similarly, Palestinian refugees supporting the PLO and HAMAS fight to regain their lost lands; Karen and other Burmese minorities sought independence or a high degree of autonomy; while Rwandan refugees wanted to retake power from their

---

[5]Personal correspondence with Indian intelligence officials, New Delhi and Kashmir, February 2001. It should also be noted that Saudi money is now going to support madrassas in Bangladesh and Nepal, which are beginning to emerge as equally important centers of recruitment for the Taliban.

hated ethnic rivals. Insurgent leaders can harness this sense of nationalism and revenge in attracting recruits or other forms of support.

Refugees may also back insurgents as a form of protection in their host country. Refugee camps are often brutal and lawless places. Such conditions certainly were prevalent among Eritrean and Tigrayan civilians displaced by civil conflict in Ethiopia and continue to be a feature among Karens and Kachins on the Thai-Burmese border. Without fighters of their own for protection, refugee populations would be vulnerable to banditry and abused by local thugs and hostile governments.

Refugees who support rebel groups are usually convinced that military action is necessary for their grievances to be heard and redressed. This sentiment is powerful because of the violence and upheaval that originally precipitated the refugee flow. The embittered Afghan villager or the Tutsi farmer driven from his land knew firsthand how their rivals had used force to achieve their aims. Accordingly, they inevitably came to believe that only brute force triumphs and that a negotiated settlement is impossible except from a position of military strength. Moreover, the suffering and deprivation refugees experience creates a strong desire for revenge, which can make negotiation difficult and achieving peaceful resolution impossible even if the other side is willing to make significant concessions.

Coercion is another factor explaining refugee contributions, particularly when rebel movements control refugee camps. Insurgents often come to dominate these sites, largely because they are well armed and organized, while the displaced population is weak and disorganized; in addition, there may be no government or aid agency capable of imposing order. In such circumstances, it is relatively easy for rebel groups to demand money, provisions, or recruits from displaced populations, even when those groups are not popular with the broader population that they claim to represent. After the Rwandan genocide and the subsequent Rwandan Patriotic Front's takeover of the country, for example, the murderous interahamwe and former Kigali government officials organized their resistance in UN High Commissioner for Refugees–run refugee camps in Zaire. They used the coercive power of their arms and their superior organizational skills to create a virtual government within the camps, exploiting international support to carry on their struggle against the Tutsi government in Rwanda. As long as the interahamwe controlled the distribution of food and otherwise acted as the de facto administrators of the camp, the mass of Hutus had little choice but to follow.

THE LIMITED RANGE OF REFUGEE SUPPORT

The support provided by refugees for an insurgency differs considerably from that provided by states or diasporas. Poor and lacking even basic resources, displaced populations can seldom offer arms or money. Even the highly successful Taliban relied on Pakistan for arms, materiel, and other basic support. What refugees can and do provide, however, is manpower, especially in the aftermath of mass refugee waves. The KLA, for example, was able to greatly expand its recruiting after Serbia launched an ethnic cleansing campaign in Kosovo in 1999, which displaced over 200,000 people—one-tenth of the enclave's inhabitants—from their homes. Over time, insurgents may additionally organize recruitment and training networks that draw on the entire refugee community as a manpower pool. This has occurred with Palestinians in Lebanon, Tutsis in Uganda, Afghans in Pakistan, and Tamils in India.[6]

As with diasporas, actions of the host nation are often critical when its populace seeks to assist insurgents in their home countries. If the state favors the refugees' cause or is too weak to impose its will, displaced communities can often act with impunity, channeling whatever assistance they can to rebel groups. Afghan refugees, for example, played a major role in the anti-Soviet struggle in large part because Pakistan strongly opposed Moscow's intervention in Afghanistan and made common cause with the anti-Soviet guerrillas. After the Soviet withdrawal, Afghan refugees played a similar role in the subsequent success of the Taliban largely because Islamabad

---

[6]In rare cases, refugees become integrated into the economy of the host nation, functioning comparable to diaspora communities. Such refugees are often useful sources of financial support for an insurgency. Palestinian refugees, for example, found work in Lebanon and Jordan—as well as in Saudi Arabia, Kuwait, and other Arab states far from Israel—and began sending their money to various resistance groups.

used the militia as a surrogate to impose its hegemony over its northern neighbor.

There have been numerous other instances where displaced populations have been used as strategic instruments in the power plays of competing regional states. The Congo, Rwanda, Burundi, Uganda, and Tanzania have all used asylum and assistance as a form of surrogate support for armed rebel movements in one another's states. Damascus has allowed (or, more clearly, has not prevented) Kurdish refugees in Syria to provide important backing to the PKK as a way of indirectly weakening Turkey. New Delhi has attempted to fulfill its border demarcation objectives with China by giving Tibetan exiles an essentially freehand to arm and train in India.[7]   And Malaysia has often been accused, by both the Philippine and Thai governments, of deliberately fomenting separatism in Mindanao and Pattani by allowing support and weapons to be channeled through displaced Muslims in Sabah and Kelanatan (see Chalk, 1997, p. 60; *The Far Eastern Economic Review*, 1995; *International Herald Tribune*, 1995; and *The Australian*, 1998).

When governments provide refugees with assistance and encourage them to back insurgents, the refugees' own cause and the government's blur. Refugee camps can become a place for insurgents to live and organize with relative impunity, while fighters may travel there to plan, train, or rest from operations. Such support is in essence a state-provided sanctuary even though government may be passively complicit.

State backing may also be inadvertent, especially if the government in question cannot control its own borders. Lebanon, for example, allowed Fatah and other Palestinian groups to operate from its territory during the 1970s, mainly because the central government could not force the movement to stop its attacks. Syria and Jordan, in contrast, succeeded in limiting Palestinian refugee support for anti-Israel efforts that did not suit either of these regimes' purposes.

As with diasporas, host countries' treatment of refugees frequently has a critical impact on the refugees' willingness to support insurgents over the long term. If the host country can provide security for

---

[7]Gunaratna (1997b), pp. 9–11. See also Hazarika (1994).

refugees on its soil, insurgents will be less able to coerce and obtain support. For economic reasons, many refugees may also prefer to assimilate into their host country rather than return to their homeland, a factor that can greatly affect support over time.

Chapter Five

OTHER NON-STATE SUPPORTERS OF INSURGENCIES

States, diasporas, and refugees are not the only sources of external support. In many of the conflicts in the 1990s, additional categories of non-state actors have helped insurgents—including other revolutionary groups, religious leaders and organizations, wealthy individuals, and human rights organizations. In general, these sources of support have strengthened and sustained insurgencies, particularly in their early days, but they have seldom had influence comparable to states, diasporas, or refugees.

Table 5.1 presents a partial listing of these various types of support. Although this breakdown should not be viewed as definitive (because data on many of these non-state actors are difficult to obtain), this compilation does raise several points. First, revolutionary groups often inspire or back insurgents elsewhere. The Lebanese Hezbollah, for example, has trained fighters from a number of Arab and Muslim groups, as has the Taliban. For many revolutionary groups, their agenda and actions are not necessarily limited to immediate theater of conflict. Second, religious organizations and influential individuals have been active backers of a number of insurgencies, particularly in the Muslim world. From the Philippines to Algeria, Islamic organizations and individual religious leaders have provided funding, inspired guerrillas with their teachings and spiritual guidance, and otherwise championed the insurgents' cause. Third, a wealthy individual can, at times, be an important financial backer of an insurgency. The individual can provide thousands or even millions of dollars and can greatly increase the resources of an insurgent

Table 5.1

Other Types of Non-State Support

Country	Insurgency Name	Other Outside Support
Afghanistan	Various small movements based on ethnicity, tribe, region, or following an individual leader	Religious organizations and individuals, wealthy individuals
Afghanistan	Taliban	Religious organizations and individuals, wealthy individuals
Algeria	Islamic Salvation Army (AIS)	Religious organizations and individuals, other revolutionary groups
Algeria	Armed Islamic Group (GIA)	Religious leaders, religious organizations, other insurgency groups
Burundi	Various ethnic Hutu groups	Former Rwandan Army (FAR) and interahamwe forces in the Congo, human rights organizations in refugee camps
Egypt	Gamaat Islamiya (IG) and other small Islamist groups	Religious organizations and individuals
Georgia	Abkhaz separatists	Volunteers from neighboring Caucasus states
India (Kashmir)	Harakat al-Ansar	Wealthy individuals and religious organizations, other revolutionary groups
India (Kashmir)	Lashkar-e Taiba	Wealthy individuals and religious organizations, other revolutionary groups
India (Kashmir)	Hizb al Mujahideen	Wealthy individuals and religious organizations, other revolutionary groups
Indonesia	Free Aceh Movement (GAM)	Other revolutionary groups, human rights organizations, wealthy individuals
Iraq	Various Shi'a insurgents	Other revolutionary groups
Israel (occupied territories)	Palestine Liberation Organization (PLO)	Inspirational religious leaders, other revolutionary groups, human rights organizations, NGOs

Israel (occupied territories)	HAMAS	Wealthy individuals and religious organizations, other revolutionary groups
Lebanon	Hezbollah	Other revolutionary groups, religious organizations, wealthy individuals
Nepal	Communist Party of Nepal (Maoist)	Other revolutionary groups
Philippines	The Moro Islamic Liberation Front (MILF)	Religious organizations and individuals, other revolutionary groups
Republic of the Congo	Various opposition groups	Other revolutionary groups
Russia	Chechen rebels	Other revolutionary groups, mercenaries, religious organizations and individuals, wealthy individuals
Sierra Leone	Revolutionary United Front (RUF)	Other revolutionary groups
South Africa	African National Congress (ANC)	Other revolutionary groups, human rights groups
Tajikistan	United Tajik Opposition	Wealthy individuals, religious organizations and individuals, other revolutionary groups
Thailand	Pattani United Liberation Organization (PULO)	Other revolutionary groups, religious organizations
Uzbekistan	Islamic Movement of Uzbekistan (IMU)	Other revolutionary groups, wealthy individuals, religious organizations

movement. Finally, human rights groups have often played a significant role in a number of conflicts throughout the globe, either indirectly by succoring fighters as well as refugees or by being co-opted by the group in question.

A case study of the influence that each of these categories of supporters has had is beyond the scope of this report. However, we do present an overview of perhaps the most important type of supporter not covered in previous chapters: one rebel group that seeks to support another. Drawing on the experience of the National Patriotic Front of Liberia (NPFL) support for the RUF, this chapter examines how a committed insurgency can spawn its own proxy group. It then, more briefly, describes the characteristics of the other non-state actors noted in the table. It concludes by arguing that the impact of these non-state actors is usually, though not always, far less significant than that of states, diasporas, or refugees.

LIBERIA AND THE CREATION OF THE RUF

In Liberia, the NPFL waged a bitter campaign of insurgency between 1989 and 1997. The group, led by Charles Taylor, gained prominence on Christmas Eve 1989 when it launched a 100-man[1] invasion to overthrow the increasingly unpopular regime of Samuel Doe. Bereft of U.S. Cold War aid,[2] lacking an effective military and bureaucracy that was capable of defending his government, and with no core constituency prepared to support his rule, Doe was unable to stymie the rapid advance of the NPFL. By June 1990, the group had approached the outskirts of Monrovia and was prevented from seizing the capital by the dispatch of the Economic Community of West African States Monitoring Group (ECOMOG) a 12,000-person multinational force based out of Sierra Leone and composed mostly of Nigerian troops.[3]

In his struggle with ECOMOG, Taylor played a crucial role in forming and then backing Foday Sankoh's RUF.[4] In 1991, the NPFL directly assisted with the launching of the first armed RUF intervention against the Freetown government, sparking the war that continues to this day. The initial incursion was staged from areas under the con-

---

[1]Taylor claimed the invasion force included 105 "trained commandos." Other officials have put the number in the attack party closer to 96. Later mythology has it that the invasion force consisted of over 150 fighters, trained and armed by Libya. See Ellis (1999), p. 75. note 1.

[2]During the Cold War, Samuel Doe's strong anti-Soviet stance earned him the vigorous support and financial backing of Washington. A total of $500 million was transferred to Liberia from the United States throughout the 1980s, making the country the largest per capita American aid recipient in Africa. See Reno (1996), p. 212.

[3]Nigeria took a leading role in ECOMOG largely as a result of the personal influence of President Ibrahim Banbangida, who was determined to stamp out rebel wars in Africa that were being fought for material and political conquest. See, for instance, *Africa News Service* (2000).

[4]Taylor and Sankoh initially became friends in the early 1980s, when both trained at a Libyan desert camp that had been set up by Colonel Muammar al-Qaddafi for African revolutionaries.

trol of Taylor's forces and subsequently supported by NPFL guerrillas as well as allied mercenaries from Burkina Faso and Cote d'Ivoire (Reno, 1999, pp. 113–114; Reno, 1996, p. 213; Riley, 1996, pp. 12–13; *The Europa World Year Book,* 2000, p. 3105; Kamara, 2000b; *Inter Press Service* 1992b, 1994a, 1996; *Periscope Daily Defense Capsules,* 1993; *Jane's World Insurgency and Terrorism,* 2000; *The Economist,* 2000e; *Periscope Daily News,* 1994).

The RUF, like insurgencies in the Congo, has little popular support. Thus, outside backing was critical for the group to survive and challenge the government. Without Taylor's initial support, it is likely that the group never would have been more than a group of local bandits. His continued support has also helped the poorly led and fissiparous RUF to maintain some unity.

Between 1991 and 1997, Sankoh's main line of support continued to be Taylor's Liberian corridor. The range of support was extensive, including arms (many of which were captured from ECOMOG troops), fighters, ammunition, communications, and intelligence. The NPFL is also believed to have provided limited tactical training, most of which took place at the group's main base headquarters at Gbarnga, in Liberia's northern region. In addition to this direct military assistance, Taylor played a key role in replenishing the RUF's spent resources and battle-incurred wastage and helped to ensure its unity under a single organizational structure.

This backing not only ensured the early survival of the RUF; it also allowed the group to rapidly develop into a genuine countrywide insurgency. Indeed, from an initial movement of some 150 combatants who were mostly confined to the south and east of Sierra Leone, the group had, by the mid-1990s, expanded to between 4,000 and 6,000 guerrillas who were capable of operating throughout Sierra Leone—including the Freetown peninsula (Carver, 1997).

The NPFL's support for the RUF was a product of several factors. Revenge and tactical considerations undoubtedly played a major role. From the outset of his own war, Taylor had become convinced that the government of Sierra Leone was his nemesis. Not only did Freetown prevent him from using the country as a corridor through which to launch his 1989 offensive; the ECOMOG intervention that prevented him from capturing Monrovia in 1990 was availed, in no small part, by the existence of a rear base in Sierra Leone. In supporting the RUF, Taylor hoped to both avenge his failure to capture the capital as well as undermine the general ECOMOG operation in Liberia thereby securing the presidency for himself (see also Riley, 1996, pp. 7, 13; Kamara, 2000a; *The Europa World Year Book*, 2000, p. 3105; *Inter Press Service* 1992a,b, 1996).

Security was also an important motivating influence. Other than the Armed Forces of Liberia and ECOMOG, Taylor faced a serious challenge from the United Liberation Movement for Democracy (ULIMO), a significant anti-NPFL militia that emerged in 1991.[5] The group mostly comprised of Krahn and Madingo Muslim refugees who had fled to Sierra Leone in an attempt to escape massacres perpetrated by NPFL guerrillas as they consolidated their control over the country in 1990. ULIMO benefited considerably from weapons and the safe haven provided by the Freetown government and was effectively employed by ECOMOG to pressure NPFL forces in northwest Liberia. Taylor hoped to offset this latent challenge through the RUF, using the group to carry out diversionary and disruptive attacks against ULIMO forces and bases located along the permeable Sierra Leone–Liberian border (Ellis, 1999, pp. 94–104; Reno, 1999, pp. 102–106; *Washington Post*, 2000b; *Inter Press Service*, 1994b).

Arguably the most important rationale for backing RUF, however, was Taylor's desire to capture the diamond fields of Sierra Leone. The Liberian leader had originally attempted to do this by working with corrupt state officials and military officers who engaged in informal trade on their side of the border. However, he realized the best way to assert control over the fields was to permanently remove any form of Sierra Leonean influence. Launching the RUF insur-

---

[5]ULIMO was formed in mid-1991 by Doe's former Deputy Minister for Information, Alhaji Kromah. In 1993, the movement split with the emergence of the so-called ULIMO-J faction, which was headed by General Roosevelt Johnson, a former AFL officer. Other anti-NPFL militias that emerged during the 1990s included the Liberian United Defense Force, an exile group founded by the former Minister of Defense, Albert Karpeh, and the Liberian Peace Council, an armed faction led by George Booley that drew support from veterans of Doe's Special Anti-Terrorist Unit. It should also be noted that two anti-Taylor factions were formed from the ranks of the NPFL itself: the Independent NPFL and the NPFL–Central Revolutionary Committee, both of which defected to ECOMOG. For further details on these various groups see Ellis (1999), pp. 94–104; Reno (1999), pp. 102–106; Butty (1992); Volman (1996); Gbala (1994); and U.S. Agency for International Development (1997), p. 1.

gency was integral to this objective. Not only did it provide Taylor with a war that effectively removed corrupt officials from the lucrative trans-border trade, it also allowed him to establish proxy rebel control over much of Sierra Leone's diamond mining and exporting business (Reno, 1999, pp. 98–99; Reno, 1996, p. 213; *The Sunday Telegraph,* 2000; *The Scotsman,* 2000; Kamara, 2000b; *The New York Times on the Web,* 2000).

THE IMPACT OF NPFL EXTERNAL ACTIVITIES

Taylor and the NPFL benefited in several ways from supporting the RUF. First, the RUF destabilized Sierra Leone, Taylor's nearest and most important regional competitor. By the mid-1990s, the war against Sankoh was consuming over three-quarters of the government's spending and had all but eliminated the country's attraction as a viable investment opportunity. The conflict was also directly responsible for the 1995 closure of the Sierra Rutile and Sierra Leone Ore and Metal Company bauxite mines, which together represented Freetown's most important source of domestic income (Reno, 1997, p. 228). Apart from economic damage, the brutal nature of the RUF campaign—the group became infamous for dismembering its victims while still alive and terrorizing noncombatants through systematic amputations—tore at the sociopolitical fabric of Sierra Leone, generating massive refugee flows and undermining the country's governing and civil institutions.

Second, by supporting the RUF, Taylor secured access to Sierra Leone's lucrative diamond fields. Prior to 1991, most of the country's gems passed through a vertical chain of intermediate buyers and sellers, typically ending with either a Lebanese or Senegalese trader who had international connections in Europe. Following the outbreak of civil war, however, the RUF—with NPFL assistance—quickly overthrew this established system of trade and inserted itself at both the bottom and top of Sierra Leone's diamond pyramid. Gems mined by the group (often by children who had been abducted for this purpose) would be directly transported across the border to Liberia and exchanged for guns. Taylor would then ship the diamonds to trading centers in Antwerp and Tel Aviv—often with the assistance of Libyan or Guinean middlemen—where they would be cut, polished, and sold (*The Economist,* 2000a). According to one nongovernmental source, Partnership Africa Canada, Taylor was earning as much as $500 million a year through this process even two years before he was chosen as president. These funds proved critical in sustaining the NPFL's war effort and helped entrench the group as Liberia's single most important and powerful faction (see *The Perspective*, 2000; Ellis, 1999, pp. 90–91; Reno, 1999, pp. 98–99; *The Sunday Telegraph*, 2000).

Finally, playing the RUF card allowed Taylor to portray the NPFL as more than a local insurgency, bolstering the group's credentials as a powerful and acknowledgeable force. This quasi-state status and powers generated increased pressure on ECOMOG's rear operating base in Sierra Leone and underscored the need to accommodate the NPFL in order to secure peace, both in Liberia, and more generally, throughout the subregion. The various peace talks and cease-fires between 1993 and 1997, all of which reserved a prominent role for Taylor's group, reflected this influence.

On the negative side, however, backing the RUF tainted the NPFL's image as a legitimate national liberation movement. Certainly the group's support for what was (and is) Africa's most-brutal rebel organization undercut potentially important political support in the West, as did its direct complicity in Sankoh's illicit diamond trade. Moreover, by establishing intimate operational and logistical links with the RUF, Taylor ensured he would be viewed as equally complicit in Sierra Leone's long-term destruction, a factor that continues to cloud his perceived international standing as Liberian president. The RUF also proved to be somewhat untrustworthy as a surrogate ally, periodically shifting alliances for its own pragmatic purposes. Occasionally these changes came at the expense of the NPFL's wider strategic interests.[6] Such instances well demonstrate the general limits of proxy control, even when the benefactor in question happens to be one as critical and "generous"—at least from the RUF's perspective—as the NPFL.

---

[6]Perhaps the clearest example of this took place in the mid-1990s, when Sankoh established a temporary "commercial" partnership with ULIMO, Taylor's main rival in western Liberia.

RELIGIOUS LEADERS AND ORGANIZATIONS

Often, religious leaders and organizations are also active supporters of revolutionary insurgent movements. This is particularly true of Islamic organizations, which primarily provide money but may also give other forms of material support as well as act as a conduit for volunteers.[7] Religious leaders have also offered intellectual support for insurgents. Rulings from clerics in Tehran have justified Lebanese Hezbollah attacks and generally promoted the organization; Algerian insurgents have found support in the writings of militant theologians in London and France; theologians in Egypt, Saudi Arabia, New Jersey, and Sudan have inspired militants as far away as the Philippines.

Religious support, like broader charitable assistance, often fluctuates with media coverage. Islamic fighters in Bosnia, Algeria, Afghanistan, and other highly publicized war zones, for instance, have received considerable support from coreligionists around the world. This assistance has become particularly evident following insurgent military success or in the wake of media-focused incidents of civil suffering.

Often this type of support occurs at the local level, with benevolent organizations and neighborhood mosques taking lead. Many Muslims consider contributions to Islamic insurgent causes to be a legitimate means of fulfilling their charitable religious obligations. They often donate to NGOs assuming that their pledges will be used to succor women and children, or otherwise relieve the humanitarian plight of Muslims in a war zone. In reality, however, these contributions often end up assisting the overall war effort.

States often tolerate and sometimes even encourage this support, worrying that any clampdown or active opposition might anger citizens who regard it as a moral duty to support their embattled coreli-

---

[7]Sendero Luminoso ("Shining Path"), for example, has received money and publicity from the Committee to Support the Revolution in Peru—an autonomous group in the United States that supports the Maoist cause. As enthusiasm for Marxist causes has waned in the last decade, so too has support from these organizations. Some insurgencies and states create front groups to channel aid and foster political support, but these front groups are a means for outsiders to provide support, not an autonomous actor.

gionists. Although the Riyadh government, for example, is concerned about the spread of Islamic radicalism to the kingdom, it has hesitated to crack down on Saudi citizens' support for radical causes abroad for fear of jeopardizing its religious legitimacy (Byman and Green, 1999, pp. 84–88). A government may also regard non-state support for an insurgency as completing or complimenting its own overall policy. Iran has encouraged public donations to Lebanese and Bosnian Muslims in addition to the aid it provides to militants abroad. Similarly, Pakistan has worked closely with non-state groups to aid both the Taliban and various Kashmiri insurgent groups; it sees this as a way to shore up domestic support while bolstering the overall effort of these two movements.

WEALTHY INDIVIDUALS

Insurgencies also receive support from wealthy individuals, motivated by ethnic affinity, religious solidarity, common ideology, or personal reasons. As noted above, many pious Muslims support a host of international Islamic causes, including insurgent movements. Similarly, a prominent medical practitioner living in California is known to have pledged as much as $4 million to the LTTE over the last decade, making him the single most important individual contributor to the group. As one former Tiger representative remarked: "We ask and he gives. [He] is our [financial] God."[8] Left-leaning donors have also occasionally provided thousands of dollars to Marxist movements, such as the Tupac Amaru Revolutionary Movement and the Sendero Luminoso, both in Peru.

AID AGENCIES AND HUMAN RIGHTS GROUPS

Aid agencies seldom deliberately assist an insurgency movement. However, their activities often indirectly channel resources to rebel groups or otherwise abet their cause. In central Africa, for example, relief groups have set up refugee camps that have become safe havens for fighters. Elsewhere on the continent, NGOs and UN agencies have provided resources to guerrillas, either directly by

---

[8]Interview with N. S. Krishnan, first LTTE European representative, London, January 1998.

working with insurgent organizations to ensure that aid reaches needy individuals or indirectly as a result of guerrilla raids on their emergency supplies (Barber, 1997, pp. 8–14). At times, insurgent organizations effectively co-opt local aid organizations. In Chechnya, for example, insurgent-affiliated NGOs promote their activities internationally as humanitarian assistance, when they are in fact working closely with guerrillas.

Human rights groups can also call attention to an insurgency's cause, increasing international support for the movement and hampering government counterinsurgency efforts. Groups celebrating indigenous rights or cultural diversity, for example, may create and foment international support for a local tribal or ethnic group. A case in point are the Zapatistas, who have become a cause celebre for many concerned groups and individuals, attracting international support from around the world. Rights groups also may accuse governments of torture, administrative detention, or other questionable tactics, which can serve to undermine the perceived legitimacy of their overall counterinsurgency efforts. This has been particularly acute with regard to Indonesia, where Jakarta has been frequently censured for human rights violations in the name of fighting separatist groups in East Timor, Aceh, and Irian Jaya. Because counterinsurgency efforts tend to be violent and brutal, human rights groups almost always, in the end, aid an insurgency by publicizing government human rights violations.

LIMITS TO SUPPORT

Sometimes the categories of non-state supporters described in this chapter have served to increase an insurgency's military power, financial position, or diplomatic influence. The NPFL's sponsorship of the RUF, for example, created a rebel group from scratch and then used it to destabilize an entire country. Such backing tends to be particularly important in the early stages of a guerrilla campaign, when the organization in question is often little more than a terrorist group with insurgent aspirations.

Overall, however, these types of supporters generally do not have the impact on insurgencies that state, diaspora, and refugees do. Even the highly organized, well-funded, and dedicated Islamist organizations usually do not provide enough assets to tip the balance of an insurgency. For example, religiously motivated volunteers swelled the ranks of various Islamist Kashmiri groups and the Taliban; however, their support paled compared to Pakistan's. In general, religious organizations, wealthy individuals, and many other non-state or non-refugee supporters are attracted to success and, thus, tend to contribute when an insurgency is already a viable entity.

ASSESSING THE IMPACT OF EXTERNAL SUPPORT

Insurgents may receive many forms of support, but the impact of this assistance varies. Some forms of support allow insurgencies to survive ferocious government onslaught or to weather a decrease in popular support. Other types, while useful, contribute far less to the overall success of the movement.

Although the impact of external support must be measured against the particular needs of and conditions facing the insurgency in question, broader generalizations can be drawn about which forms of assistance are usually the most important to insurgent movements. Chapter Six provides a brief overview of guerrilla movement requirements and notes how outside powers can help meet these needs. It divides these contributions into those that, in our judgment, are critical, those that are valuable, and those that are minor. This chapter also discusses the political, organizational, and operational costs associated with a group's acceptance of outside support.

INSURGENT REQUIREMENTS

To be successful, insurgent movements have a variety of requirements, most of which can be grouped in two categories—human and material. In general, insurgents most need outside support of all kinds when they cannot obtain this support domestically. Insurgent requirements are summarized in Table 6.1. Each requirement is discussed in more detail below.

Table 6.1

Insurgent Requirements

Human	Material
Ability to mobilize local and international support	Safe haven and transit
Capable leadership, including effective command and control	Financial resources
Training	Direct military support
Intelligence concerning the adversary	Arms and materiel, including ammunition, food, and fuel
Inspiration	
Organizational aid	

CRITICAL FORMS OF SUPPORT

Safe Haven and Transit

Safe havens, whether inside the country where the insurgents operate or across international boundaries, are essential to the success of
any guerrilla movement. Sanctuaries protect the group's leadership
and members; provide a place where insurgents can rest, recuperate,
and plan future operations; serve as a staging area from which to
mount attacks; and, in some cases, function as an additional base for
recruitment, training, dissemination of propaganda, and contact
with the outside world. Such sanctuary allows guerrillas and their
commanders to organize, train, recruit, plan, recuperate, and
otherwise conduct essential operations outside the reach of the targeted state. Without a safe haven, insurgencies are constantly vulnerable to government forces. Iraqi Shi'ites, for example, have been
able to organize themselves and receive essential military training in
Iran—activities that would have been impossible in Iraq given
Saddam Husayn's tight controls. Safe havens also allow insurgents
to dictate the pace of operations, prevent target governments from
following up tactical victories when they are denied the right of "hot
pursuit," and otherwise help rebel movements retain their initiative.
Kashmiri militants, for instance, often reside in Pakistan until the
weather, local political conditions, and other factors are conducive to
launching cross-border initiatives and attacks.

During a number of recent conflicts, cross-border sanctuaries appear to have been a major contributor to insurgent effectiveness, particularly when counterinsurgent forces are highly capable. For example, part of the success of the ANC relative to the Pan-African Congress (PAC) can be explained because the ANC had access to safe havens in Mozambique, where militants could train, rest, and plan future operations. The PAC, on the other hand, had no external sanctuaries, and thus was forced to confront highly competent and aggressive South African security forces without being able to recuperate in the comparative safety of a frontline state. The PKK's access to sanctuaries in Syria and the Syrian-controlled Beka'a Valley in Lebanon during the 1980s and early 1990s permitted the movement to thrive; the withdrawal of Syrian support a decade later consequently played a major role in the PKK's collapse (Radu, 2001, p. 52). In South Asia, Nepalese Maoist insurgents routinely use India as a sanctuary, which also serves as a base for political, logistical, and financial support of the movement (*IISS Strategic Comments,* 2000, p. 2; Santina, 2001, pp. 34–37). Relative geography, of course, is important; international safe havens are most useful when they are across contiguous borders.

Sometimes neighboring states provide insurgents with a haven simply because they are incapable of ousting the rebels themselves. Thus, the IMU has a de facto haven in Tajikistan because Dushanbe does not control its borders. Similarly, Lebanon for many years hosted a variety of Palestinian groups that targeted Israel mostly because the central government in Beirut was too weak to defeat them militarily (Hiro, 1992, pp. 81–110).

Some insurgencies may also be able to create a safe haven within the boundaries of the state in which they are fighting. Groups that enjoyed strong support in particular regions, such as the Chinese communist guerrillas led by Mao, are often able to have tremendous freedom of action, and even create alternative government institutions, in part of a country. Geography, again, also plays a role: Sendero Luminoso, for example, took advantage of Peru's mountains and jungles, creating a liberated zone in parts of Peru.

Refugee camps also function as a form of safe haven—one that usually requires the support, or at least acquiescence, of the host state. Insurgent movements use these sites to organize, train, recruit, acquire arms, and otherwise advance their cause. As noted above, this most often occurs when the host government favors the refugee cause or is otherwise too weak to control the activities of the displaced populations on its territory (or when the international community creates a sanctuary). Refugee camps may also serve as safe havens, particularly if international organizations help create them, making it difficult politically for government forces to attack there. In such cases, refugee camps are liable to become safe places for the combatants' dependents, a base for organizing, and a source of food and shelter for fighters.

The existence of a contiguous guerrilla safe haven often leads a civil war to escalate into a larger interstate conflict. Government troops cross borders to attack insurgent camps and bases. In so doing, they often confront border forces, air defense assets, and other state security units protecting or providing insurgents with assistance. Escalation may also occur when government forces have punished the sponsoring state directly. Israel regularly held sovereign backers of Palestinian groups responsible for insurgents' cross-border attacks, using this to justify raids against a wide range of targets in the host country. The Israeli defense forces attacked targets in Egypt, Lebanon, and Jordan—and on occasion as far afield as Tunisia. This reciprocal pattern of insurgent support and Israeli response greatly contributed to overall Arab-Israeli tension and helped spark the 1956 Suez Crisis and 1967 Six-Day War (Morris, 1994, pp. 340–418, 429–431).

The right to transit relates to the possession of a safe haven. When rebels can transit neighboring states (either through the connivance of an allied government or because of its weakness) it becomes far harder for their adversaries to defeat them. In some instances, a state may also permit insurgents to transit a country or receive support from another backer indirectly. Syria has allowed Iran to send soldiers to Lebanon and funnel weapons to Hezbollah through its territory, while the Zagreb government permitted Bosnian Croats and Muslims to receive arms that were destined for insurgent forces via Croatia. Such support is often a low-cost form of assistance, allowing the transiting state to control the aid flow and even sometimes to divert it, while still maintaining some distance from the insurgent cause.

Financial Resources

Money has a powerful effect on insurgent movements: It can be used to buy weapons, bribe local officials, pay operatives, write propaganda, provide a social network that builds a popular base, and otherwise fulfill myriad purposes. Insurgents are often able to acquire some of what they need via theft or from local supporters. However, they also require cash to acquire safe houses, procure weapons and ammunition, pay bribes, meet legal expenses and, in some cases, to pay stipends to militants. As J. Bowyer Bell (1998, p. 138) has noted, "money is a real and persistent problem. The movement commanders must pay their way, pay for the prisoners' families, pay for newsprint. . . . There seldom seems enough money."

Some of these funds can be generated internally, through bank robberies, kidnappings, and in the case of Sendero Luminoso in Peru and Colombia's FARC, through "revolutionary taxes" imposed on drug traffickers. But given that most insurgencies take place in impoverished areas, guerrilla movements often are forced to look abroad for funds they need to support their armed struggle. States can supply money, but in the post–Cold War era, diasporas and foreign sympathizers have also proven to be important sources of cash. In some instances, insurgent movements have become self-financing, at least in part. Such financing can take the form of legitimate business enterprises abroad, such as small-scale "mom and pop" shops selling items such as T-shirts and jewelry. A number of insurgencies, such as the RUF in Sierra Leone, Cambodia's Khmer Rouge, and the Turkish PKK, also have engaged in highly profitable illicit activities, including arms trafficking, gem smuggling, and the transportation of illegal immigrants.

States often play a critical role in funding insurgencies. Hezbollah is an excellent example. The group has used Iranian financial support, conservatively estimated at $100 million a year, both to maintain its fighting strength and to create a vast socioeconomic network for its supporters, a combination of which has greatly enhanced its prestige and influence (Ranstorp, 1997, pp. 33–48, 78–86).

In contrast to safe havens, which are primarily offered by states, diasporas often can provide considerable financial assistance while creative insurgent groups can at times finance themselves. Funds given by diasporas, both voluntarily and through extortion, and wealthy individuals have been vital to the success of the LTTE, the PIRA, Sikh militants, and the mujahedin, to cite a few examples. Through a combination of fundraising, legitimate businesses, and illicit enterprises, the organizations have been able to generate staggering sums sufficient to bankroll their armed struggles almost indefinitely. LTTE revenues are estimated at $48–72 million a year, while UNITA is estimated to generate $80–150 million per year, largely from diamond smuggling and other illegal ventures.[1] These figures were dwarfed by those for the PKK, which during the height of its power in the mid-1990s was generating an estimated $200–500 million annually (Radu, 2001, p. 55). Such sums are even more impressive considering they will be spent primarily in economically underdeveloped areas of the world, where U.S. dollars, British pounds, German deutschmarks, and other hard currencies have a powerful impact.

Political Support and Propaganda

State patrons often provide important political support for insurgent movements. Cataloguing the entire range of this type of backing is beyond the scope of this study. However, this span includes everything from giving insurgents access to the state's diplomatic apparatus and pushing for recognition in international fora, to encouraging aid agencies to provide assistance to the group directly, to otherwise underwriting insurgent causes by portraying and lobbying for them as a legitimate voice of a particular people or ideology. Moreover, political support often involves denying assistance to the government the insurgents oppose. Diasporas at times indirectly contribute to state political support, using their electoral or financial clout to encourage their host governments to back an insurgency or oppose government counterinsurgency campaigns.

Political support often has important consequences both seen and unseen. Arab and Muslim countries have long backed the Palestinian cause, using their influence to gain aid dollars for displaced persons and refugees; to press other countries to boycott Israel; to

---

[1]During the mid-1990s, the LTTE reportedly was banking an estimated $650,000 a month in Switzerland alone (Davis, 1996a).

encourage recognition of the PLO as the legitimate voice of the Palestinian people; and otherwise to place Palestinian grievances on the international agenda. In this way, the Palestinian cause engaged the superpowers during the Cold War, remaining a staple feature of regional politics even though the Palestinian movement itself was relatively weak militarily. In contrast, although the Taliban's military successes have led it to dominate over 90 percent of Afghanistan, the combined opposition of Russia, the United States, Iran, China, and other adversaries of the movement have continually deprived it of recognition as Afghanistan's legitimate government and blunted Taliban efforts to obtain seats in international organizations.

Of course, the level of political support depends on both the state's commitment to the insurgent movement and the power it generally wields. The backing of a major power can, for example, hamstring UN attempts to contain or defeat a rebel movement. Russian support of the Serb cause in the Balkans is an especially notorious recent case. Pakistan, by contrast, has so far failed to gain wide recognition or support for either the Taliban or the various Kashmiri insurgent groups its sponsors largely because Islamabad lacks Moscow's diplomatic clout.

In our judgment, political support is particularly critical once an insurgency is established. Weak rebel groups rarely receive more than token political support. Outside governments or diaspora groups, however, may champion more successful insurgent causes. This may involve recognizing the insurgents as a legitimate government, pressuring the regime they are battling and denying them access to weapons of money, or otherwise trying to give the insurgency access to the benefits of being a legitimate political entity while denying the same to their adversary. Such support assists the insurgents in material terms (more aid, a weaker adversary) and politically, by demonstrating to their followers that resistance is succeeding while undermining support for the state.

Propaganda is a critical instrument for generating political support and fundraising for every contemporary insurgent movement, both within its theater of operations and among a broader international audience. Effective propaganda can help legitimize insurgent goals, aid in fundraising and recruitment activities, discredit opposing governments, and internationalize the armed struggle by bringing a movement's message to a broader audience.

States often assist insurgents in generating propaganda, helping rebel groups portray themselves as innocent victims who deserve assistance, as pious Muslims worthy of financial support, as devoted socialists, etc. Outside support can help make insurgent propaganda more potent in at least two ways. First, external actors can provide the technical expertise and resources that underground groups lack. States may provide insurgents with useful access to radio, television, the Internet and other media through which they can effectively spread their message. Second, and more important, sympathetic states, front groups, ideological sympathizers, and diaspora members can serve as transmission belts for insurgent propaganda. Governments battling insurgencies are likely to find it far more difficult to control the propaganda activities carried out by proxies, supporters, and state sponsors across international borders.[2]

Although states continue to support their proxies with propaganda, non-state actors have become much more significant sources of this type of assistance in recent years. Across the world, front groups and ideological sympathizers publish newspapers, books and magazines, and maintain web sites aimed at promoting insurgent causes.[3] In some cases, as with the PKK, sympathizers have operated radio and television stations designed to further their respective movements. The precise impact of positive publicity and propaganda is difficult to gauge; however, it does appear that such assistance remains a vital element in the success of many of post–Cold War insurgencies, not

---

[2]During the Cold War, the Soviet Union and the United States frequently aided insurgencies by helping them develop and transmit propaganda. Statements by important foreign leaders expressing support for an insurgency or its goals played an important part of superpower propaganda campaigns on behalf of their guerrilla proxies, and such support was strongly associated with the success of insurgent campaigns during the Cold War (Defense Systems, Inc., 1986, p. 36). The study analyzed 132 campaigns drawn from 15 insurgencies during 1945–1981. Fourteen types of assistance, ranging from cadre training to heavy military equipment, were identified. Of these 14 forms of assistance, propaganda, international recognition, and financial aid were determined to be "very strongly associated with campaign success" (pp. 35–36).

[3]Most insurgencies of any consequence, such as the FARC, the LTTE, and the Kurdish underground movements, aggressively use the Internet to promote their cause, particularly internationally. For typical examples of insurgent web sites, see www.ozgurluk.org; www.contrast.org/mirrors/farc; and www.eelam.com.

least by legitimating a group and its cause and augmenting its general ability to fundraise abroad.

Direct Military Support

States at times provide direct military support, using their own armies to fight alongside insurgents. Not surprisingly, such direct assistance is rare, but when it occurs it usually has a tremendous impact on the fighting. The Taliban, the Bosnian Croats, the Abkhaz, the forces of Laurent Kabila, pro-CIS forces in Tajikistan, and several other insurgent movements have all gained an outright victory over their rivals—a relatively rare phenomenon in the annals of insurgency—largely because of the backing of neighboring state military forces. Without this support, it is likely that these movements would have been completely defeated or, at best, would have clung to survival in the face of superior state forces.

Outside military forces fundamentally change the nature of an insurgency's struggle. No longer is it a battle of guerrillas against armies while rival institutions compete for the loyalty and cooperation of the populace. When states step in, the confrontation becomes more comparable to interstate war than civil conflict. Armies fight directly in conventional clashes, while guerrilla conflict often assumes secondary importance. The level of weaponry increases tremendously, from small arms to advanced air and land systems. The insurgents also are far more likely to be able to conduct massive and coordinated conventional attacks, enabling them to occupy territory, outgun and outmaneuver rival forces, and otherwise conduct operations that were previously beyond their capabilities.

In general, state forces are better armed, organized, and led, and typically more able to conduct sophisticated operations. As a result, the scope and scale of insurgent capabilities can increase exponentially, allowing previous weak groups that simply sought to survive to develop into a genuine security threat. The Congo experience illustrates how potent direct intervention can be. Before Kabila obtained Rwandan and Ugandan backing, he was an obscure guerrilla leader who posed little danger to the Zairian regime. With the support of troops from Kigali and Kampala, however, Kabila quickly began to pose a direct threat to the Mobutu regime, eventually overthrowing it and installing himself as president of the newly constituted

Democratic Republic of the Congo. When Kabila became less responsive to the needs of Rwanda and Uganda, the two countries acted to remove their former puppet—and would have succeeded had it not been for the timely intervention of other states, including Zimbabwe and Angola.

VALUABLE FORMS OF SUPPORT

Training

To become effective on the battlefield, militants must be given weapons training and instruction in small-unit tactics. Although this is often provided by the militants themselves, the relevant training skills are not always available in-house. On some occasions, insurgents must turn to outsiders for support. Particularly in the early days of a conflict, the group may lack a cadre of skilled, experienced fighters who can pass on their knowledge to new recruits. In addition, training is often required in the case of more-specialized techniques, such as terrorist tradecraft, small-unit tactics, and the use of more-exotic weapons—such as man-portable air defense systems or, as has been alleged in the case of training camps operated in Afghanistan, chemical weapons (Miller, 2000, p. 1). As is the case with external manpower support, such assistance can help bolster the legitimacy and credibility of an insurgent movement by demonstrating the commitment of outsiders.

Pakistan stands out as a country particularly active in training insurgent groups. Islamabad's assistance, provided through the ISI, is rudimentary, according to public accounts, and consists primarily of training recruits in the use of explosives and small arms such as the AK-47 (Kanwal, 1999, pp. 55–83). However, Indian sources claim that supplemental training is far more advanced and includes instruction in advanced explosive skills, forced entry attacks, intelligence tradecraft, and other difficult skills. Similarly, Iranian Islamic Revolutionary Guard Corps units helped transform Hezbollah from a rag-tag group of poorly armed terrorists to one of the world's most formidable insurgent movements. Tehran's forces instructed Hezbollah guerrillas on a variety of weapons systems, intelligence gathering, and conducting small-unit attacks. Given that many insurgent movements face state militaries that are often poorly equipped and unmotivated, even limited increases in armed effectiveness can have an impressive payoff vis-à-vis enemy government forces.

Non-state groups have also supplied training assistance. Hezbollah, often acting as Iran's surrogate, has trained Islamic insurgents and terrorists who are active throughout the Muslim world. Indian Maoists, for example, reportedly have provided military training to communist insurgents operating in Nepal (*IISS Strategic Comments,* 2000, p. 2).

It appears, however, that the most effective insurgent groups are self-taught. As a movement develops, it is able to create cadres who in turn train new recruits. In certain parts of the world, such as Latin America, insurgencies in their formative stages also have included former soldiers who have been able to impart their military skills to fellow combatants.

Once a group has mastered the fundamentals of waging an insurgency, it becomes a candidate for training in more-advanced tactics, techniques, and procedures. In Afghanistan, members of Usama bin Laden's Al Qaeda ("The Base") organization reportedly have trained Islamist militants in specialized techniques such as counter-intelligence, kidnapping, and urban guerrilla operations.[4]

Weapons and Materiel

Small arms are any insurgency's defining technology. During the Cold War, the United States and the Soviet Union often helped their proxies meet logistical requirements by supplying weapons and equipment. Many smaller states also provided weapons to underground movements during the Cold War. In the mid-1980s, for example, Libya supplied hundreds of rifles and handguns and more than 2,500 kg of Semtex explosive to the PIRA, which gave the organization the ability to sustain its terrorist campaign on a virtually indefinite basis.[5] But even in the periods of the most sustained super-

---

[4]Engelberg (2001), p. 13. According to one published account, 50,000 to 70,000 militants from 55 countries have been trained by Al Qaeda in Afghanistan (Miller, 2000).

[5]Horgan and Taylor (1999), p. 5; O'Callaghan (2000). O'Callaghan was a former commanding officer in the PIRA's Southern Command.

power assistance, insurgents were sometimes compelled to obtain arms with little or no assistance from their patrons. In El Salvador, for example, insurgents used weapons captured from the army, bought on the black market, or obtained through sophisticated bartering with East European or African countries (Radu and Tismaneanu, 1990, p. 192).

In some respect, the end of the Cold War has created a worldwide surplus of small arms that made such weaponry both more plentiful and cheaper (see Rana, 1995). Guerrillas usually are also able to acquire some of what they need through theft; raids on police, paramilitary, and army outposts; from corrupt members of the security forces or sympathizers within their ranks; or from adversaries who simply leave their weapons behind after an attack. Materiel, including ammunition, food, and fuel, usually is readily available, either by theft, purchase, or from supporters.

Fortunately for insurgents with financial resources, international arms markets are brimming with small arms, and governments often have, at best, limited control over their borders, particularly if they are facing a strong insurgency.[6] Gunaratna (2000a) has described one important source of weapons for Asian-Pacific militant organizations:

> The economic decline in former Soviet bloc countries meant that financial rather than security considerations determined the sale of weapons. As a result, some [groups] gained access to automatic weapons and explosives at competitive prices. Similarly, access to dual technologies—GPS [global positioning systems], satellite imagery, radar, secure communication, computers, sea scooters, speed boat[s], microlights and drones—enabled terrorist groups to challenge previously formidable land and naval forces.

The illicit international market for small arms such as assault rifles, machine guns, and shoulder-fired missiles is worth $2–10 billion a year, according to a 1998 estimate (*IISS Strategic Comments,* 1998, p. 1). This vast armaments bazaar has become an option for those insurgents whose local sources are inadequate. While some groups continue to receive weapons and equipment from state and non-

---

[6]For a review, see Boutwell and Klare (1999).

state sponsors, the existence of such markets means that insurgents are not necessarily compelled to turn to outside patrons for arms and other supplies.

In some circumstances, however, external provision of arms and materiel is quite valuable. Certainly, when local dealers do not have access to the full range of hardware and equipment sought by guerrillas, outside assistance is valuable. In addition, weapons provided by outsiders free rebel groups to spend their scarce funds on other needs. Moreover, in campaigns against capable counterinsurgent forces, it may be difficult for insurgents to acquire weapons without outside support. Security services may monitor borders and local markets and closely scrutinize local military forces to avoid illicit weapons diversions. At times, the police and army may be less willing to sell their weapons. In these cases, insurgents may turn to state or non-state sponsors, or may seek to buy weapons on international markets that are beyond the reach of the adversary's security forces.

MINOR FORMS OF SUPPORT

Fighters

Skilled, dedicated, and experienced fighters are the fundamental requirement of any successful rebel movement. By definition, insurgencies are protracted political-military campaigns involving the use of irregular forces. To achieve their objectives, insurgent movements need sufficient numbers of motivated combatants capable of performing credibly against government security forces and in some cases, anti-insurgent paramilitary entities. Recruiting suitable manpower will be a concern at each stage of the insurgency. If government forces are proficient, they will inflict casualties. Counterintelligence operations, psychological operations, civic action, and other components of a well-crafted and well-executed counterinsurgency effort are also likely to deplete guerrilla ranks. Even when counterinsurgency efforts are poor, arrests, defections, simple exhaustion and, in some cases, diminished commitment to the cause will also serve to reduce the number of combatants.

Foreigners often directly aid insurgents by providing additional manpower to supplement native insurgents. Conflicts in Bosnia, Chechnya, Dagestan, Kashmir, and Kosovo, have all seen an influx of guest Islamic militants, many of whom have acted as a crucial anchor for fighting that occurs on the ground (Foreign Broadcast Information Service, 2000). The participation of foreign combatants contributes to the insurgents' goal of internationalizing their armed struggle and provides additional manpower to the native insurgents (see Engelberg, 2001, p. 1). The involvement of guest militants offers concrete evidence that these insurgencies are more than mere local conflicts, but were part of a regional or global campaign on behalf of Islam. Sometimes personnel with particularly rare skills (e.g., computer programming, demolitions) may be lacking from the local manpower pool.

In general, rebel groups seldom rely on outsiders for manpower, and those that do risk disaster.[7] If an insurgency cannot attract fighters, it is often a sign that the movement is poorly led or does not have a message that appeals to enough people. In addition, local combatants are often far more adept at providing intelligence, gaining access to materiel, or otherwise helping sustain the movement. Seldom are large numbers of outside fighters available to most insurgencies; they represent at best a limited manpower pool. Finally, outside volunteers may be fickle and move on to another insurgency if it suits their goals and needs. Even when the outsiders are refugees or from a diaspora, they may be out of touch with local conditions and attitudes. The PLO, for example, was long criticized for its perceived aloofness from the struggle in the West Bank and Gaza Strip.

For many insurgencies, however, the costs of extensive participation from outside militants may sometimes outweigh their benefits. For example, a large influx of foreign combatants can erode the credibility of a nationalist or separatist movement. Outsiders may also bring with them attitudes and behavior that harm the insurgent cause. Indian sources claim that early mujahedin militants participating in the Kashmir conflict were undisciplined; they alienated local population through acts of extortion and other forms of abuse (Grau and Jalali, 1999, pp. 66–71). Such abuses, like any human rights viola-

---

[7]This characterization excludes direct intervention by a state's military forces on behalf of an insurgency (e.g., Rwanda's intervention in the Congo or Russia's intervention in Tajikistan). In such cases, foreign support replaces the insurgency itself rather than augmenting it.

tions involving insurgent forces, carry the additional possibility of undermining the movement's legitimacy in the eyes of current and potential supporters abroad. In addition, foreign combatants often have different goals than local fighters (e.g., spreading Islam versus self-determination), which can create internal dissension or dispute.

Intelligence

To be effective, it is essential for any insurgent movement to understand the nature, objectives, and capabilities of its adversaries. This understanding includes the size and composition of security forces, the strengths and weaknesses of the opposition's leadership and strategy, and the level of the population's support for the underground movement as well as the government. In some instances, insurgents may turn to outsiders to provide intelligence that is difficult or costly to acquire themselves. The RUF, for example, received intelligence from the NPFL that helped in its struggle with Freetown.

Outside provision of intelligence, however, is seldom decisive and often of only limited value.[8] With most movements, the insurgents themselves have better information on local conditions than any outside sponsors or supporters could provide. In any clandestine movement, members are also part-time intelligence agents, operating among the population, gathering information, and conveying it to higher authorities. Insurgents typically are able to draw on a large network of informants and local sympathizers who can provide information useful to the cause. Many movements, according to Bell (1999, p. 159), have been able to rely on "a spy in the castle, a policeman with a rebel heart, a clerk with access to the needed files. . . . The facts are there for those who will invest time and take a risk. The shoeshine boy outside the presidential palace sooner or later will find out something useful."

---

[8]This generalization does not always hold. For some insurgencies, intelligence support provided by outside actors has been a contributor to the effectiveness of political-military campaigns. In Kashmir, for example, direct tactical intelligence supplied by Pakistan's ISI reportedly has given Islamist militant groups an increased capability that has helped drive the conflict with India to a near stalemate (Evans, 2000, p. 78).

In short, insurgent groups are able to acquire much of the intelligence they need on their own. Insurgents, because of their access to sources in the area of conflict, are most likely *suppliers* of information to external supporters rather than *recipients* of intelligence from outside actors.[9]

Organizational Aid

When outsiders help an insurgency organize, the group is often better able to attract recruits, sustain operations, or otherwise perform basic functions essential to long-term success. Such assistance is particularly important in the early days of an insurgency. Iran and the Lebanese Hezbollah, as previously noted, are an example of such a case. With somewhat less success though, Iran also pushed various Afghan Shi'a factors to unite into the Hezb-e Wahdat organization, increasing their overall clout and effectiveness. Islamist groups helped HAMAS organize, and various Arab states assisted in the creation of the PLO.

Governments often provide insurgent groups with organizational aid that takes many forms: attempts to broker deals among different organizational factions, assistance with recruitment, provision of financial incentives to encourage cooperation among opposition rivals, dissemination of lessons learned from previous insurgencies, and facilitation of propaganda. The United States, for example, has helped Iraqi groups unite under the banner of the Iraqi National Congress, lending at least a nominal coherence to their anti-Saddam efforts (Byman, 1999, pp. 23–37). Iran has also assisted Hezbollah in setting up a vast support network that provides recruits, intelligence, funds, and influence in Lebanese politics. Equally, the backers of various highly fractious Afghan movements helped them form the NA in 1996, solidifying and integrating opposition to the Taliban.

Strong insurgencies, however, must soon organize themselves or face serious risks. The Lebanese Hezbollah, for example, retained close ties to Iran but has steadily began to manage its own affairs and

---

[9]In the northeastern Indian state of Assam, for example, the separatist United Liberation Front of Assam has reportedly provided its ISI sponsors with information on Indian troop movements from the northeast to the western and northern borders with Pakistan (Bedi, 2000, p. 32).

operations. As a result, it has become a far more effective actor on the local political scene, able to tailor its operations—and at times rein them in—to improve the group's local popularity. Similarly, both HAMAS and the PLO became effective actors in part because they distanced themselves from the organizations that initially backed them, ensuring that local officials managed their affairs.

Inspiration

Inspiration from abroad often helps get an insurgent movement off the ground, but seldom sustains it for long. Marxism, Islamic radicalism, and other transnational credos have often inspired insurgents, encouraging them to resist government and transform society. In addition, the success of an ethnic group in advancing its cause in one country can convince other organizations in the same country or in neighboring areas that they can change their status in society and that violence can be an effective tool (Lake and Rothchild, 1998, pp. 25–27).

Sometimes a state's rhetoric or experience will inspire insurgents even when other forms of aid are limited. Such indirect support can demonstrate the viability of armed resistance, offer a particular organizing model, or illustrate the force of ideas. The Iranian revolution, for instance, inspired Muslim militants worldwide. Even though many Sunni militants opposed Iran's Shi'a government and distinct Islamic credo, the example of religion as a potent means to overthrowing a despotic authoritarian regime led a host of Sunni Muslim organizations to try to emulate Iran's revolution as a useful model.

Even when it does not materialize, the hope of outside backing can make rebellion more likely. A state's rhetorical support, for example, may inspire rebels to take a stand, believing that assistance is forthcoming. In such circumstances, potential insurgents may believe that the costs of resistance will be few and the promise of success more real (Lake and Rothchild, 1998, pp. 26–27). This type of inspiration is often deadly. Although outside promises may lead insurgents to remain firm in the face of government pressure, they can also cause them to avoid compromise and engage in costly provocations, even when facing probable defeat.

Over time, insurgents must develop an ideology and message that has local appeal. A blind commitment to a transnational ideology may inspire fighters for a time, but will inhibit indigenous recruitment and prevent a movement from capitalizing on local opportunities. Although a successful revolution or other heady success can increase the attraction of a particular ideology, its popular appeal almost invariably fades with time.[10] A failure to go beyond foreign inspiration therefore equals disaster for any insurgent movement's potential longevity.

As the above review makes clear, insurgents' requirements vary tremendously. The assistance insurgents receive thus varies in value according to the needs of the particular group and its struggle. Almost all groups can benefit from a safe haven and diplomatic assistance. Some groups, however, do not need foreign assistance to buy arms because they can be obtained locally. Others may require training, while some can train themselves. In gauging the effects of outside assistance, it is critical to recognize that its value is directly related to what insurgents can and cannot acquire by themselves.

THE COSTS OF EXTERNAL SUPPORT

For insurgents, assistance from external sponsors entails costs as well as benefits. As noted above, foreign manpower, while helping to fill depleted guerrilla ranks, can also lead to a loss of nationalist credibility and, if human rights abuses occur, an erosion of local and international support. A large influx of cash to insurgents can contribute to corruption, feuding, and internal discord, as with the Afghan and Nicaraguan resistance forces during the 1980s (Bonner, 1987, p. 342). Foreign assistance in the form of international sanctuaries, while often extremely useful to guerrillas, can also have a negative impact. In moving abroad, insurgents risk cutting themselves off from their base of popular support. Resting and recuperating across a border, while providing obvious benefits, also carries the danger of operational isolation from potentially lucrative political and military targets (Laqueur, 1998, p. 393). Other forms of assis-

---

[10]For a discussion of this phenomenon with regard to radical Islam, perhaps the most potent transnational ideology today with the exception of liberal democracy, see Roy (1994).

tance, such as the provision of weapons, can have a distorting and negative effect on an insurgency's military tactics.[11]

An alliance with a foreign power can also lead to more-violent government crackdowns on the insurgents or their perceived civilian supporters. The government and its domestic supporters are more likely to view the insurgents not simply as rebels, but as traitors. This is especially true if the government fighting the insurgency is also battling an international war with state supporters of the insurgents. Such associations contributed to mass killings of Kurds in Iraq, who had worked with Iran during the Iran-Iraq war. Previously in history, Turkish fear of Armenian collusion with Russia during World War I was a major impetus behind the Armenian genocide.

More broadly, external aid can lead to a decrease in an insurgency's freedom of action. Outside patrons typically seek some measure of control in exchange for their political, financial, and logistical investments (Bell, 1999, p. 166). However, insurgents—particularly those driven by strong nationalist sensibilities—generally are reluctant to allow their movement to fall under foreign domination.[12] Movements and their patrons often find themselves at odds over questions of strategy and tactics, political objectives, and the tempo and nature of political-military operations.

External support can also be fickle. Typically, second-generation members of diasporas are less enthusiastic about armed struggles than are their elders, and so fundraising by insurgents within those communities may prove to be more difficult over time. The LTTE, for example, is beginning to experience increased difficulty raising funds among younger members of the overseas Tamil community, many of whom have been absorbed into their host societies and retain little, if any, affinity for the Eelam cause (Ranetunge, n.d.).

---

[11]During the 1980s, for example, the Afghan resistance had ready access to foreign-supplied longer-range weapons, such as 82-mm mortars and 107-mm rockets. As a result, resistance forces were able to minimize their own casualties by conducting frequent long-range barrages. However, such barrages were often ineffective against Soviet forces, and came at the expense of more potentially fruitful operations designed to take ground or defeat adversary units (Isby, 1992, p. 207).

[12]Rice (1988), p. 78. However, it should be noted that in some cases, such as Kashmir, the state sponsor has found it extremely difficult to exercise authority over its client (Bose, 1999, p. 163).

In some instances, a dependency on state sponsors can have devastating consequences. A regime's goals and priorities are likely to change over time, and in some cases, a state will abandon an insurgency to take advantage of new strategic opportunities. Iran, for example, has both supported and reined in Iraq's SAIRI, varying its backing according to its geopolitical needs. Thus, Iran pushed SAIRI to undertake often-ruinous operations during its eight-year war with Iraq but provided, at best, tepid backing in 1991 when Saddam's regime was reeling following the Gulf War. Despite Saddam's weakness, Tehran wanted to avoid even an appearance of meddling in order to deprive the U.S.-led coalition of a pretext for continued intervention in Iraq, or even in Iran itself.

As important as external support can be to a guerrilla movement, it can also impose damaging and unacceptable burdens on an underground organization. In ideological, religious, and nationalist insurgencies, militants are risking their lives, and possibly those of their friends and families, to further a set of beliefs. Thus, self-reliance, dedication to the struggle, and self-denial are extremely useful qualities in rebel groups. Excessive reliance on foreign assistance can undercut these virtues and diminish the martial capabilities of a guerrilla movement, as demonstrated by the PLO's poor performance against the Israeli military after years of comfortable sanctuary in Syrian-controlled Lebanon. As insurgency analyst Gerard Chaliand (1987, p. 58) has cautioned, "every seriously organized guerrilla movement is well advised to rely mainly on its own resources."

In general, dependence on refugees, diasporas, and other non-state supporters carries fewer risks for insurgencies, even though the type of support these actors can provide is limited. Diasporas and refugees tend to follow the lead of rebel movements rather than view them as temporary allies or proxies to be controlled. As a result, sudden changes in funding or political support are far less likely.

Chapter Seven

IMPLICATIONS FOR THE ANALYSIS OF INSURGENCY

This final chapter reviews several of the most important findings of this report and discusses their implications for intelligence analysts and policymakers. It begins by briefly reviewing the obvious lesson from the previous analysis: Outside support for insurgency today differs fundamentally from the Cold War period. It then attempts to distinguish which types of external assistance have the most impact. This chapter concludes by arguing that passive support is an important but often ignored form of backing that allows many movements to flourish.

MOVING BEYOND THE COLD WAR

The indomitable Viet Cong guerrilla, adhering to a tight discipline while he plays his part in a coordinated assault on the South, the UNITA leader in his Western-style "Tiger" camouflage, and the Afghan mujahedin brandishing a Stinger anti-aircraft missile all color our perception of who an insurgent is. But these images mislead. The analysis presented in the previous chapters suggests that insurgency is displaying a different face today than it did during the Cold War. The PKK, the LTTE, and the Lebanese Hezbollah all are as potent as, or perhaps even more impressive than, the superpower proxies of the Cold War even though they lack superpower support.

The new sponsors, including new state patrons, are different in their means and objectives from Cold War superpowers. In contrast to the United States and the Soviet Union, most state supporters' motivations are local in nature. Gaining influence in a neighboring region or with a rival government are leading objectives, as opposed to contributing to the triumph of a particular ideology or global alliance bloc. Even Moscow, which before the end of communism backed guerrillas in Latin America and Africa as well as in Asia, now uses support for insurgents primarily to gain influence in its immediate neighborhood. In addition, most of the states that remain active supporters of guerrilla movements (e.g., Pakistan, Rwanda, and Iran) are relatively poor and unable to support large-scale insurgencies far from their borders without placing a serious burden on their already-limited finances.

The most important shift that has taken place, however, is the rise in importance of non-state actors, particularly diasporas but also refugees, insurgent movements that sponsor other movements, and religious organizations. States still can offer a far wider range of support than non-state actors, but in several instances, non-state actors have played a major role in funding and otherwise sustaining insurgencies.

Figure 7.1 reviews the relative contributions of different types of outside supporters. As the figure suggests, states provide a far wider range of support and thus can be the most valuable backers of an insurgency. Insurgencies, however, can receive valuable assistance from several other types of outside backers.

DISTINGUISHING AMONG INSURGENCY STAGES

Measuring the impact of outside support is difficult, because its value is always relative. Insurgents seek externally what they cannot acquire internally: One movement may need a haven; another, weapons; and a third, political support. The value of these types of support thus varies with the particular requirements of the insurgent movements. Moreover, the value of external support depends heavily on the existing strength of a movement. Money given to a poor insurgent movement often has a greater impact than money given to a wealthy one. Similarly, strong insurgencies may receive more support than weaker ones, but the support has only a marginal benefit to the strong while it may be essential to the weaker group. Because the importance of outside support is also relative, the scale of this support does not always correspond with its significance to the insurgency.

RAND MR1405-7.1

Form of Support	States	Diasporas	Refugees	Other Non-state
Money	Significant	Significant		Minor
Safe Haven	Significant		Minor	Minor
Diplomatic Backing	Significant	Limited		
Arms	Significant	Minor		Limited
Training	Significant	Minor		Minor
Intelligence		Minor		
Direct Mil Support	Significant		Limited	Minor
Inspiration	Limited	Minor		Minor

Significant contribution   Limited contribution   Minor contribution

Figure 7.1—A Comparison of External Actors' Contributions

The impact of outside support depends greatly on the stage of an insurgency. Outside supporters, even wealthy individuals, can have a tremendous impact at the initial stages of an insurgency. Before an insurgency becomes well established, the relative balance between government forces and those of the insurgents tends to heavily favor the regime. Having a haven from which to organize, a source of arms and money, and protection from the regime's intelligence services— alongside other forms of more tangible aid—can help an insurgent movement survive a government's initial onslaught. Outside support can also enable a group to gain the upper hand on its rivals within the overall resistance. Often, initial resistance consists of scattered and disorganized bands of fighters. Outside support can enable one group to be better armed, trained, and funded: All attract more fighters and thus further increase a group's edge over its rivals. As previously noted, success breeds additional support, creating a positive cycle for the insurgent group. The publicity generated from an insurgent success—or simply from being the group best known to the outside world—makes it more likely that the group will receive aid.

States, however, can often make a difference in helping an insurgency triumph over its government opponent. Particularly when the regime it opposes is weak, it is often easier for a rebel movement to seize a remote region of a country and even undermine government control more broadly. Taking control of the entire country, however, invites many complications. The insurgents must be able to defeat government forces and impose their own rule—a qualitative increase in capabilities from mere subversion. The insurgent movement frequently must acquire more-sophisticated arms, be able to conduct conventional military operations as well as guerrilla attacks, govern large swathes of territory and ensure their economic viability, and otherwise fight and act in a completely different manner from that of a small movement living off the land. In addition, a government may gain additional support as neighboring states and other concerned parties increase their aid in order to prevent an insurgent victory. While money and fighters provided from diasporas, refugees, and other supporters can help in this effort, state support is often necessary to help insurgents reach a new level of political and military effectiveness. Not surprisingly, the majority of insurgencies that have won outright military victories had the strong backing of at least one state—including direct military assistance from that state's armed forces.

THE IMPORTANCE OF PASSIVE SUPPORT

Sometimes a state's passivity has more of an impact than any formal support it may provide. Diasporas and other interested outsiders often openly raise money, distribute propaganda, and otherwise aid an insurgency's cause with little interference from a host government even when that government generally opposes the insurgents and favors the government they are fighting. It remains relatively easy for many illicit organizations to operate abroad, particularly within democratic states, where concerns about civil liberties, diaspora political pressure, and other factors have led to a de facto toleration for insurgent fundraising activities (Chalk, 2000c). Certainly the PKK, the LTTE, and HAMAS, among others, have successfully exploited their respective diasporas and other well-wishers in the West to gain important funding and propaganda assistance.

Similarly, refugees are sometimes able to organize and freely support an insurgent movement with little interference. The initial assumption that refugees deserve international support often blinds governments and international organizations to their active role in an ongoing conflict. Sometimes the international community engages in acts of willful blindness, refusing to recognize what relief workers and local fighters on the ground know well: Aid can fuel or prolong fighting, as well as alleviate suffering.

One of the most important forms of outside support, the provision of a safe haven, often occurs because of a state's weakness rather than its deliberate policy. When states cannot control their borders or exercise effective control over isolated parts of the country, insurgents often flourish. In parts of Central Asia, much of Africa, and elsewhere, insurgents can escape their government adversaries and organize freely.

FINAL WORDS

This report has attempted to describe general trends in outside support for insurgent movements and assess their impact. However, a wide range of challenges remain for insurgency analysts. Although this discussion provides a first step that analysts can expand upon and advance in their work, most of the qualitative judgments rendered here are relative: Different factors matter at different times and have different effects according to the strength of government, terrain, overall balance of forces, and a host of other factors. It is therefore imperative that the impact of outside support be considered within the context and contours of a particular conflict environment and measures as part of an overall net assessment of the insurgency's strength, relative to that of the government.

Analysts must also move outside the traditional, country-based focus when assessing insurgencies. The LTTE, for example, depends on a network that ranges from Canada to Thailand; Hezbollah works with Lebanese Shi'a in the triple border area of Argentina, Paraguay, and Brazil; the Kurds depend heavily on Kurdish workers in Europe; etc. Analysts must assess whether a host government controls or regulates refugees and diasporas in its territory in order to assess the likelihood of which forms of support will be used—an assessment that requires combining knowledge of different regions. Because passive support is so important, analysts must look at what is *not* done as well as track the flow of arms, money, volunteers, and other active forms of support.

OUTSIDE SUPPORT FOR INSURGENCIES (1991–2000)

Table A.1

Outside Support for Insurgencies (1991–2000)[a]

Country	Insurgency Name	Significant or Critical State Support and Identity of State[b]	Significant Refugee Support	Significant Diaspora Support	Significant Other Outside Support
Afghanistan	Taliban	Pakistan	Yes		Yes
Afghanistan	United Islamic Front for the Salvation of Afghanistan (UIFSA) or Northern Alliance	Iran, Russia, Uzbekistan	Yes		
Afghanistan	Various small movements based on ethnicity, tribe, region, or following an individual leader	Pakistan, Russia, Uzbekistan, Iran, Saudi Arabia	Yes		Yes
Algeria	Islamic Salvation Army (AIS)			Yes	Yes
Algeria	Armed Islamic Group (GIA)			Yes	Yes
Angola	National Union for the Total Independence of Angola (UNITA)	South Africa, Tanzania, Zambia, Namibia			
Azerbaijan	Armenian separatists in Nagorno-Karbakh	Armenia, Russia		Yes	
Bosnia	Bosnian Croats	Croatia			
Bosnia	Bosnian Serbs	Serbia			
Burma	Karen National Union (KNU)		Yes		
Burundi	Conseil National de Defense et de Democratie (CNDD) and its armed wing, the Forces pour la Defense de la Democratie (FDD) and other ethnic Hutu groups	Tanzania	Yes		Yes

Table A.1—continued[a]

Country	Insurgency Name	Significant or Critical State Support and Identity of State[b]	Significant Refugee Support	Significant Diaspora Support	Significant Other Outside Support
Cambodia	Khmer Rouge—Party of Democratic Kampuchea	China			
Colombia	National Liberation Army (ELN)				
Colombia[c]	Revolutionary Armed Forces of Colombia (FARC)				
Croatia	Serb revolt in Krajina	Serbia			
Democratic Republic of the Congo	Pro-Kabila forces who defeated Mobutu Sese Seko	Rwanda, Uganda			
Democratic Republic of the Congo	Rassemblement Congolais pour la Democratie (RCD-Kisangani)	Uganda	Yes		
Democratic Republic of the Congo	Rassemblement Congolais pour la Democratie (RCD-Goma)	Rwanda	Yes		
Democratic Republic of the Congo	Mouvement de Liberation Congolais (MLC)	Uganda	Yes		
Egypt	Gamaat Islamiya (IG) and other small Islamist groups			Yes	Yes
El Salvador	Farabundo Marti National Liberation Front (FMLN)				

Table A.1—continued[a]

Country	Insurgency Name	Significant or Critical State Support and Identity of State[b]	Significant Refugee Support	Significant Diaspora Support	Significant Other Outside Support
Ethiopia	Oromo Liberation Front (OLF)	Eritrea, Somalia	Yes		
Georgia	Abkhaz separatists	Russia			
Georgia	South Ossetian separatists	Russia			
Guatemala	Various leftist groups				Yes
Guinea Bissau	Antigovernment organizations				
India	United Liberation Front of Assam and other groups in Assam				
India	National Front for the Liberation of Bodoland				
India	Punjabi separatists	Pakistan		Yes	
India (Kashmir)	Hizb al Mujahideen	Pakistan		Yes	Yes
India (Kashmir)	Harakat al-Ansar	Pakistan		Yes	Yes
India (Kashmir)	Jammu and Kashmir Liberation Front (JKLF)	Pakistan		Yes	
India (Kashmir)	Lashkar-e-Taiba	Pakistan		Yes	Yes
Indonesia	East Timor Guerrilla resistance				
Indonesia	Free Aceh Movement (GAM)			Yes	Yes
Iran[d]	Mujahedin-e Khalq (MEK)	Iraq			
Iraq	Kurdistan Democratic Party (KDP)	Iran, U.S.			
Iraq	Patriotic Union of Kurdistan (PUK)	Iran, U.S.			

Table A.1—continued[a]

Country	Insurgency Name	Significant or Critical State Support and Identity of State[b]	Significant Refugee Support	Significant Diaspora Support	Significant Other Outside Support
Iraq	Various Shi'a insurgents	Iran	Yes		Yes
Iraq[e]	Iraqi National Congress (INC)	U.S.			
Israel (occupied territories)	Palestine Liberation Organization (PLO)	Various Arab states, wide political support	Yes	Yes	Yes
Israel (occupied territories)	HAMAS	Iran, Gulf states	Yes	Yes	Yes
Lebanon	Hezbollah	Syria, Iran		Yes	Yes
Liberia	National Patriotic Front (NPFL) and associated factions (Charles Taylor)	Libya			
Mexico	Zapatistas (or Ejercito Zapatista de Liberacion Nacional [EZLN])				
Moldova	Trans-Dniester guerrillas	Russia			
Mozambique	Mozambican National Resistance (RENAMO)	South Africa			
Nepal	Communist Party of Nepal—Maoist				Yes
Peru	Tupac Amaru Revolutionary Movement (MRTA)				
Peru	Sendero Luminoso				
Philippines	The Moro Islamic Liberation Front (MILF)				Yes
Philippines	The Moro National Liberation Front (MNLF)				
Republic of the Congo	Various opposition groups	Angola	Yes		Yes

Table A.1—continued[a]

Country	Insurgency Name	Significant or Critical State Support and Identity of State[b]	Significant Refugee Support	Significant Diaspora Support	Significant Other Outside Support
Russia	Chechen Rebels		Yes	Yes	Yes
Rwanda	Rwandan Patriotic Front (RPF)	Uganda	Yes	Yes	
Rwanda	Forces Armees Rwandaises (ex-FAR)	Kabila government	Yes	Yes	Yes
Senegal	Movement of Democratic Forces in the Casamance (MFDC)	Guinea-Bissau	f	f	f
Sierra Leone	Revolutionary United Front	Liberia	Yes		Yes
South Africa	African National Congress (ANC)	Various frontline African states			Yes
Sri Lanka	Liberation Tigers of Tamil Eelam (LTTE)		Yes	Yes	Yes
Sudan	South Sudan Independence Movement/Army (SSIM/A)		Yes		
Sudan	National Democratic Alliance—comprises several opposition organizations, of which Sudan People's Liberation Movement is the largest		Yes		
Tajikistan	United Tajik Opposition				Yes
Tajikistan	Pro-CIS forces	Russia, Uzbekistan			
Thailand	Pattani United Liberation Organization (PULO)	Malaysia			Yes

Table A.1—continued[a]

Country	Insurgency Name	Significant or Critical State Support and Identity of State[b]	Significant Refugee Support	Significant Diaspora Support	Significant Other Outside Support
Turkey	Kurdish Workers Party (PKK)	Syria, Iraq		Yes	
Uganda	Allied Democratic Forces (ADF)		Yes[f]		
Uganda	Lord's Resistance Army (LRA)	Sudan			Yes
United Kingdom[g]	Provisional Irish Republican Army			Yes	
Uzbekistan	Islamic Movement of Uzbekistan (IMU)				Yes
Western Sahara	Polisario Front	Algeria			
Yugoslavia (Former)	Kosovo Liberation Army (KLA)	U.S. and NATO allies	Yes	Yes	
Yugoslavia (Former)	Slovene secessionists				
Yugoslavia (Former)	Croatian secessionists				

[a]External support provided before 1991 is excluded. Thus, even though India played a major role in developing the LTTE during the 1980s, it is not included as a state sponsor because its support ended prior to 1991.

[b]This column does not list minor state supporters, which are noted in Table 2.1.

[c]Venezuela supports the FARC but probably did not reached the "significant" threshold by the end of 2000, though it appears likely to have attained this level in 2001.

[d]The MEK sometimes conducts cross-border guerrilla operations, but its activities increasingly involve terrorism only.

[e]The INC is included because of its importance to the United States. It arguably controlled territory before the 1996 Iraqi thrust into northern Iraq.

Table A.1—continued[a]

[f] Level of support is not clear.

[g] The PIRA has territorial aspirations, but its actual control was often limited in duration and practice. The Real IRA, which split off from the PIRA after the 1998 Good Friday peace agreement, is clearly a terrorist group.

THE LTTE's MILITARY-RELATED PROCUREMENT

The Liberation Tigers of Tamil Eelam (LTTE) have a sophisticated external support network to procure weapons and acquire munitions. This is perhaps the most secretive of the group's international operations and the one that best demonstrates the organization's global reach.

Prior to 1987, the LTTE obtained the bulk of its weaponry directly from India. During the latter part of the 1970s and the first seven years of the 1980s, New Delhi played a key role in supporting the militant Tamil struggle in Sri Lanka, backing both the LTTE and several other groups such as the People's Liberation Organization of Tamil Eelam, the Eelam People's Revolutionary Liberation Front, and the Tamil Eelam Liberation Organization. This support was a product of wider ideological and geopolitical concerns, particularly Colombo's increasingly close relationship with the West and reluctance to remain under the auspices of India's nonaligned (and largely pro-Moscow) orbit. Supporting groups like the LTTE was seen as means of coercing the Sri Lankan government away from this stance. Most assistance was coordinated by the Research and Analysis Wing—the agency charged with advancing India's covert foreign policy goals—and included both insurgent training[1] and the provision of arms.

---

[1] By mid-1987, some 20,000 militants had received military training in India. Most of this instruction took place in paramilitary camps located in Tamil Nadu, although specialized courses were also run in New Delhi, Bombay, and Vishakhapatnam. The militant who assassinated Rajiv Gandhi in 1991 was trained in such a camp. For further details see Gunaratna (1997a), pp. 11, 17–19. For an analysis of the early covert activities of the Indian intelligence services, see Raina (1981).

In 1987, the Indian government reversed its policy on the insurgency in Sri Lanka, terminating all foreign assistance to Tamil militants operating in the northeast country.[2] The growing violence of the LTTE armed campaign was causing a major refugee problem throughout the southern reaches of the subcontinent[3] and encouraging secessionist sentiments in Delhi's own province of Tamil Nadu. The sudden loss of Indian backing forced a major reassessment by the LTTE with regard to arms procurement, compelling the group to seek alternative sources further afield.[4] For the past 14 years, these efforts have focused mostly on accessing weapons from markets in Eastern Europe; Southeast, Northeast and Southwest Asia; and, most recently, southern Africa.

The LTTE international arms network is headed by Tharmalingham Shunmugham, alias Kumaran Pathmanathan and colloquially known simply as "KP." One of Prabhakaran's most trusted lieutenants, he is currently the second most wanted man in Colombo. Notably nondescript in person, fully adept at working undercover and with some 20 passports reportedly to his name, Pathmanathan is known to travel broadly and has been linked by both Western and Sri Lankan intelligence sources to arms deals that have ranging from Croatia to South Africa. His main operating bases have been Rangoon, Bangkok, and, most recently, Johannesburg, with most of his transactions financed through established bank accounts held in

---

[2]This commitment was made as part of the so-called Indo–Sri Lankan Peace Accord, which aimed to bring about a negotiated settlement to the insurgency in Sri Lanka by providing for a general cease-fire and the devolution of local powers of governance for an autonomous northeastern Tamil province. An Indian Peacekeeping Force (IPKF) was dispatched to Sri Lanka to oversee guerrilla disarmament and provide security for local administrative council elections. The LTTE refused to accept the accord and, three months after it was signed, launched a major campaign against the IPKF, eventually forcing its withdrawal in March 1990 (by which time 1,155 troops had been killed and 2,987 injured). The LTTE regarded the Indian reversal as an unforgivable act of treachery; it was the major factor that influenced Prabhakaran's decision to have Rajiv Gandhi assassinated in 1991. Personal correspondence with Sri Lankan intelligence officials, Bangkok, December 2000. See also Manoi Joshi (1996) pp. 25–26; and Samaranayake (1997), pp. 115–116.

[3]By 1987, an estimated 13,000 Tamil refugees had fled to southern India.

[4]It should be noted that the LTTE managed to make up for some of the loss by stepping up indigenous weapons production (by 1991, the group had developed its own short-range missile capability) as well as carrying out increasingly daring raids against Sri Lankan military field depots.

Germany, the Netherlands, Norway, the United Kingdom, and Canada.

Most members of the LTTE global weapons procurement team, known as the "KP Department," have received no formal military training and have not been involved in violent militant operations on the ground. This reliance on noncombatants is a deliberate tactic that is designed to minimize the possibility that those involved with the highly critical task of weapons procurement will be known to either Sri Lankan or overseas intelligence and law enforcement agencies.

It is believed that Pathmanathan establishes his brokers and inter-mediaries around the world through a sophisticated human export ring that draws on the LTTE's general human-smuggling capabilities. Tamil expatriates who are already residents in states such as Australia, Canada, and the United States allegedly obtain visas for overseas countries (where such applications are less likely to arouse suspicion). Potential agents with somewhat similar facial features of the original applicants are then chosen and travel, with a LTTE representative, to the selected states. The impersonators are left to apply for refugee status (either in the chosen state or an adjacent country), while the LTTE "chaperone" returns with the original passports, handing them back to their rightful owners. According to Sri Lankan intelligence officials, this method can be repeated numerous times (with different original visa applicants), taking KP personnel to any Western country.[5]

At the heart of the KP Department's operations is a highly active shipping network, known informally within the group as the "Sea Pigeons." Although the origins of the LTTE's maritime capability go back to the early-to-mid-1980s, most development occurred following the 1987 termination of external Indian support. Today, the fleet numbers at least 11 deep-sea freighters, the majority of which reportedly sail under Honduran, Liberian, or Panamanian flags of

---

[5]Personal correspondence with Sri Lankan intelligence operative, Scotland, May 1998. Similar modus operandi were described to the author during interviews with officials at the Sri Lankan High Commission, Bangkok, December 2000. See also *The Globe and Mail* (1998b).

convenience.[6] The LTTE has exploited the lax registry requirements of these countries, allowing the group to confound international tracking and monitoring attempts by repeatedly changing the names, manifest details, and duty statements of the various vessels used. Ninety-five percent of the time these ships are involved in the legitimate transport of commercial goods such as tea, rice, paddy, fertilizer, and cement. However, for the remaining 5 percent, they play a pivotal role in supplying explosives, arms, ammunition, and other war-related materiel to the LTTE theater of conflict.[7]

As noted above, these weapons originate from a variety of sources. The booming post–Cold War arms bazaars that have emerged in Southeast and Southwest Asia form the bedrock for much of the group's overseas procurement activity, especially in Cambodia,[8] Myanmar, and Afghanistan,[9] where the group has obtained everything from rapid-fire pistols and assault rifles to rocket-propelled grenades and surface-to-air missiles. Ammunition requirements— including mortar, artillery, and 12.7-mm machine-gun rounds—are mostly met by purchases from Bulgaria, the Czech Republic, and

---

[6]It should be noted that the Sea Pigeons also sail under other flags. The *Sun Bird* (a.k.a. the *Illiyana, Francis,* or *Ichulite*), the *Amazon,* and the *Golden Bird* (a.k.a. the *Baris, St. Anthony, Sophia,* or *Parhan*), for instance, are respectively known to have been registered in Cyprus, New Zealand, and Malta.

[7]Personal correspondence with Australian Federal Police (AFP) intelligence personnel, Canberra, September 1998. See also Winchester (1998), p. 39; Gunaratna (1997b), p. 27; *The Sunday Times (Sri Lanka)* (1999); and *India Today* (1996). Although LTTE ships are rarely seized, the group has suffered some significant losses to its maritime network. Among the more important have been the *MV Cholakeri,* which capsized off the Thai coast November 28, 1992; the *Ahat* (a.k.a. the *Yahata*), which was destroyed January 16, 1993; the *Horizon,* which was destroyed February 14, 1996; the *Stillus Limmasul,* which was (eventually) destroyed November 2, 1997; and the *Blue Dawn,* which was seized off the Canadian west coast November 4, 1998.

[8]Until recently, it was possible to buy an AK-47 on the Cambodian black market for as little as 1,000 Thai baht, with bullets costing a mere 5 baht apiece. Heavier weaponry such as grenade launchers and antiaircraft missiles were priced in 1995 at 3,000 and 200,000 baht each, respectively. See Lintner (2000); and *The Bangkok Post* (1995). For a good overview of the illicit trade in small arms in Cambodia see Nonviolence International Southeast Asia Office (1998).

[9]Many of the weapons acquired from Afghanistan had initially been supplied by the United States in support of the mujahedin insurgency against the Soviet-backed regime of Babrak Karmal. One study estimates that by 1987, some 65,000 tons of munitions were being transferred each year to the Afghan rebels via Pakistan. For further details see Chalk (2000a), pp. 10–11; Chris Smith (1993), pp. 3–13; Chris Smith (1995), pp. 583–589; Krott (2000) pp. 35–39; and *The Economist* (1994).

North Korea, while explosives and related material are typically acquired from the Ukraine and Croatia.[10]

The LTTE has been pushing to extend the reaches of its global arms network to South Africa. The country lies adjacent to two of the most prolific munitions sources on the African continent, Mozambique and Angola[11] and, because of sanctions imposed during the apartheid era, has a long tradition of covert arms dealing. In addition, there is a relatively advanced communication and transportation infrastructure in place as well as the existence of several groups that are openly supportive of the Tamil liberation struggle in Sri Lanka.[12] These considerations, together with a rapidly deteriorating internal political and security environment, have combined to make South Africa particularly conducive to the establishment of a thriving underground arms trade, something the LTTE has been both quick to recognize and keen to exploit.[13]

Thailand has emerged as the main logistical interface between these various international weapons sources and the Tamil separatist war in Sri Lanka.[14] As Anthony Davis (2000), a journalist specializing in Asian security matters, observes:

---

[10]Personal correspondence with *Jane's Intelligence Review* Asia-Pacific security specialist, Bangkok, December 2000. See also Lintner (2000); *The Bangkok Post* (n.d.); *Jane's Sentinel Pointer* (1996); and *Gulf News* (1997).

[11]Arms dealers can purchase an AK-47 assault rifle, together with a couple of clips of ammunition, for as little as $14 in Mozambique, or simply exchange a bag of maize for one. It has been estimated that as many as 6 million AK-47s remain at large in the country. See Chalk (2000a), p. 11; Smith and Vines (1997), pp. 13–20; and *The Sunday Times (South Africa)* (1995).

[12]Prominent among these are the Dravidians for Peace and Justice, the Tamil Eelam Support Movement, People Against Sri Lankan Oppression, and the Movement Against Sri Lankan Oppression.

[13]See *The Sunday Times (Sri Lanka)* (1998); *Lanka Outlook* (1998b); *The Hindu* (1998a,b,c); and Gunaratna (1998b). Although the Pretoria government has given assurances to Sri Lanka that the LTTE would not be allowed to open any official offices in the country, it is not apparent how such a pledge can be enforced. South Africa has annulled all apartheid-era legislation dealing with terrorism and has not adopted any new statutes in its place. This means that a group such as the LTTE, even if formally identified as a terrorist organization, could not be prevented from openly and legitimately functioning in the country.

[14]The LTTE is thought to have been operating out of Thailand for most of the 1990s, though it is only during the last five years that the country emerged as the key hub in the group's international arms network. Prior to this, the Tigers had relied on bases off

A nation where plentiful foreign tourists and businessmen make blending in easy, [Thailand] provides access to several former war zones and their surplus weaponry. It offers excellent communication and a short sea hop across the Bay of Bengal to Sri Lanka. And as elsewhere in the region, money can [also] buy cooperation [and silence] in high places.[15]

In most cases, weapons are delivered (by the Sea Pigeons) to LTTE bases located off the southern Thai seaboard. From here they are off-loaded onto smaller vessels for the final 1,900-km trip to Tiger-controlled drop-off points along the Sri Lankan northeastern coast including Mullaitivu and the remote beaches near Batticaloa and Trincomalee.

---

the coast of Burma, moving most weapons through the island of Twante where, through preexisting ties with the military-dominated government, the group had managed to consolidate a semipermanent presence. In 1996, however, this site had to be abandoned following intense diplomatic pressure on Rangoon by Sri Lanka, leading to the establishment of alternative trafficking centers in Thailand. Personal correspondence with *Jane's Intelligence Review* Asia-Pacific security specialist, Bangkok, December 2000.

[15]See also Lintner (2000).

REFERENCES

Adeyemi, Segun, "Congo's Chaotic Peace Process," *Jane's Intelligence Review*, June 2000.

Ayoob, Mohammed, "The Security Problematic in the Third World," *World Politics*, Vol. 43, No. 2, January 1991.

Barber, Ben, "Feeding Refugees, Or War?" *Foreign Affairs*, Vol. 76, No. 4, July/August 1997.

Bedi, Rahul, "India's Never-Ending Ethnic Insurgencies," *Jane's Intelligence Review*, June 2000.

Bell, J. Bowyer, *Dragonwars: Armed Struggle and the Conventions of Modern War*, New Brunswick, N.J., and London: Transaction Publishers, 1999.

_____, *The Dynamics of the Armed Struggle*, London and Portland: Frank Cass Publishers, 1998.

Blaufarb, Douglas, *The Counterinsurgency Era: U.S. Doctrine and Performance*, New York: Free Press, 1977.

Bonner, Arthur, *Among the Afghans*, Durham, N.C., and London: Duke University Press, 1987.

Bose, Sumantra, "Kashmir: Sources of Conflict, Dimensions of Peace," *Survival*, Vol. 41, No. 3, Autumn 1999.

Boutwell, Jeffrey, and Michael T. Klare, eds., *Light Weapons and Civil Conflict*, New York: Carnegie Commission on Preventing Deadly Conflict, 1999.

Butty, James, "What Does ULIMO Want?" *West Africa*, September 7, 1992.

Byman, Daniel, "Proceed with Caution: U.S. Support for the Iraqi Opposition," *The Washington Quarterly*, Vol. 22, No. 3, Summer 1999.

Byman, Daniel L., and Jerrold D. Green, *Political Violence and Stability in the States of the Northern Persian Gulf*, Santa Monica, Calif.: RAND, 1999.

Byman, Daniel, and Stephen Van Evera, "Why They Fight: Hypotheses on the Causes of Deadly Conflict," *Security Studies*, Vol. 7, No. 3, Spring 1998.

Carver, Richard, "Sierra Leone: From Cease-Fire to Lasting Peace?" *REFWORLD*, January 1997, accessed via http://www.unhcr.ch/refworld/country/writenet/wrisle.htm.

Central Intelligence Agency, *Guide to the Analysis of Insurgency*, Washington, D.C.: Central Intelligence Agency, n.d.

Chaliand, Gerard, *Terrorism: From Popular Struggle to Media Spectacle*, London: Saqi Books, 1987.

Chalk, Peter, "Gray Area Phenomena in Southeast Asia: Piracy, Drug Trafficking and Political Terrorism," *Canberra Papers on Strategy and Defence* 123, 1997.

_____, *Non-Military Security and Global Order: The Impact of Extremism, Violence and Chaos on National and International Security*, London: Macmillan, 2000a.

_____, "Liberation Tigers of Tamil Eelam's (LTTE) International Organization and Operations: A Preliminary Analysis," *Commentary*, No. 77, Canadian Security Intelligence Service, March 17, 2000b, accessed at http://www.csis-scrs.gc.ca/eng/comment/com77e.html.

Collier, Paul, and Anke Hoeffler, "Greed and Grievance in Civil War" *Policy Research Working Papers*, The World Bank, May 2000.

Cordovez, Diego, and Selig S. Harrison, *Out of Afghanistan: The Inside Story of the Soviet Withdrawal,* New York: Oxford University Press, 1995.

David, Stephen, *Choosing Sides: Alignment and Realignment in the Third World,* Baltimore: Johns Hopkins University Press, 1991.

Davis, Anthony, "Tamil Tiger International," *Jane's Intelligence Review,* Vol. 8, No. 10, October 1996a, accessed at http://fore.thomson.com.

_____, "Tiger International," *Asiaweek,* November 26, 1996b.

_____, quoted in "Tracking Tigers in Phuket," *Asiaweek,* June 16, 2000.

Davis, Anthony, "How the Taliban Became a Military Force," and Ahmed Rashid, "Pakistan and the Taliban," both in William Maley ed., *Fundamentalism Reborn? Afghanistan and the Taliban,* London: C. Hurst, 1998.

Defense Systems, Inc., *The Role of External Support for an Insurgent Movement: Final Report,* McLean, Va.: Defense Systems, Inc., September 25, 1986.

Eckstein, Harry, ed., *Internal War: Problems and Approaches,* New York: Free Press, 1964.

Ellis, Stephen, *The Mask of Anarchy,* New York: New York University Press, 1999.

Engelberg, Stephen, "A Network of Terror: One Man and a Global Web of Violence," *New York Times,* January 14, 2001.

The Europa World Year Book 1999, "Sierra Leone," (London: Europa Publications, 2000).

Evans, Alexander, "The Kashmir Insurgency: As Bad as It Gets," *Small Wars and Insurgencies,* Vol. 11, No. 1, Spring 2000.

Fearon, James D., and David D. Laitin, "Explaining Interethnic Cooperation," *American Political Science Review,* Vol. 90, No. 4 December 1996.

Foreign Broadcast Information Service (FBIS), "Global Analysis: Is there an Islamist Internationale?" March 7, 2000, FBIS document number GMP20000712000174.

Frantz, Douglas, "Guerrilla Attacks Raise Worries in Central Asia," *New York Times*, September 6, 2000.

Gbala, Bai, "Gbala on ULIMO's Ethnic Feud," *New Democrat*, Vol. 1, No. 30, April 1994.

Goodwin-Gill, Guy, and Ilene Cohn, *Child Soldiers: The Role of Children in Armed Conflict*, Oxford: Clarendon Press, 1994.

Gourevitch, Philip, "Forsaken," *The New Yorker*, September 25, 2000.

Grau, Lester W., and Ali A. Jalali, "Kashmir: Flashpoint or Safety Valve?" *Military Review*, Vol. 79, No. 4, July/August 1999.

Gunaratna, Rohan, *International and Regional Security Implications of the Sri Lankan Tamil Insurgency*, Colombo: Bandaranaike Centre for International Studies, 1997a.

_____, "Illicit Transfer of Conventional Weapons: The Role of State and Non-State Actors in South Asia," paper presented before the Third Intersessional Workshop of the Panel of Governmental Experts on Small Arms, Kathmandhu, May 22–23, 1997b.

_____, "LTTE Child Combatants," *Jane's Intelligence Review*, July 1998a.

_____, "LTTE in South Africa," *Frontline*, December 13, 1998b.

_____, *Dynamics of Diaspora-Supported Terrorist Networks: Factors and Conditions Driving and Dampening International Support*, Ph.D. thesis, University of St. Andrews, Scotland, October 1999.

_____, "Terrorists Threats Target Asia," *Jane's Intelligence Review*, July 1, 2000a, accessed at http://fore.thomson.com.

_____, "LTTE Organization and Operations in Canada," unpublished document supplied to author, November 2000b.

Harden, Blaine, "Africa's Gems: Warfare's Best Friend," *New York Times*, April 6, 2000.

Hazarika, Sanjoy, *Strangers in the Mist: Tales of War and Peace from India's Northeast,* New Delhi: Viking-Penguin, 1994.

Hiro, Dilip, *Lebanon: Fire and Embers,* New York: St. Martin's Press, 1992.

Hoffman, Bruce, *Inside Terrorism,* New York: Columbia University Press, 1998.

Horgan, John, and Max. Taylor, "Playing the 'Green Card'—Financing the Provisional IRA: Part 1," *Terrorism and Political Violence,* Vol. 11, No. 2, Summer 1999.

Horowitz, Donald, *Ethnic Groups in Conflict,* Berkeley, Calif.: University of California Press, 1985.

Howard, Shawn, "The Afghan Connection: Islamic Extremism in Central Asia," *National Security Studies Quarterly,* Summer 2000.

Huth, Paul K., *Standing Your Ground: Territorial Disputes and International Conflict,* Ann Arbor, Mich.: The University of Michigan Press, 1996.

Isby, David C. "Afghanistan: Low-Intensity Conflict with Major Power Intervention," in Edwin C. Corr and Stephen Sloan, eds., *Low-Intensity Conflict: Old Threats in a New World,* Boulder, Colo.: Westview Press, 1992.

Joshi, Charu, "The Body Trade," *The Far Eastern Economic Review,* October 26, 2000.

Joshi, Manoi, "On the Razor's Edge: The Liberation Tigers of Tamil Eelam," *Studies in Conflict and Terrorism* 19, 1996.

Kamara, Tom, "Charles Taylor Defends Sankoh," *The Perspective,* May 2000a.

_____, "Will Taylor Join Sankoh Before the Tribunal?" *The Perspective,* July 31, 2000b.

Kanwal, Gurmeet, "Proxy War in Kashmir: Jihad or State-Sponsored Terrorism?" *Strategic Analysis,* Vol. 23, No. 1, April 1999.

Kelly, William, and John Bryden, *The Report of the Special Senate Committee on Security and Intelligence,* Ottawa: Senate of Canada, January 1999.

Khalizad, Zalmay, Daniel Byman, Elie Krakowski, and Don Ritter, *U.S. Policy in Afghanistan: Challenges and Solutions,* White Paper prepared for the Afghanistan Foundation, 1999.

Kizito, Sabala, *State Forces and Major Armed Opposition Groups in the Great Lakes Region of Africa* (Nairobi: Africa Peace Forum, January 1999), accessed via http://www.fewer.org/greatlakes/glreb99.html.

Krott, Rob, "Guns of the Other Frontier," *Soldier of Fortune,* January 2000.

Lake, David A., and Donald Rothchild, "Spreading Fear: The Genesis of Transnational Ethnic Conflict," in *The International Spread of Ethnic Conflict: Fear, Diffusion, and Escalation,* Princeton, N.J.: Princeton University Press, 1998.

Laqueur, Walter, *Guerrilla Warfare: A Historical and Critical Study* New Brunswick, N.J., and London: Transaction Publishers, 1998.

Lawless, Richard, and Laila Monahan, eds., *War and Refugees: The Western Sahara Conflict,* New York: Pinter, 1987.

Leites, Nathan, and Charles Wolf, Jr., *Rebellion and Authority: An Analytic Essay on Insurgent Conflicts,* Chicago: Markham, 1970.

Lemarchand, Rene, "The Fire in the Great Lakes," *Current History,* May 1999.

Lintner, Bertil, "The Phuket Connection," *The Week,* April 30, 2000.

LTTE Atrocities, internal document supplied to author, December 2000.

Lynch, Colum, "U.S. Warns Liberia Again on Its Support for Sierra Leone Rebels," *Washington Post,* August 3, 2000.

Machel, Graca, *Impact of Armed Conflict on Children,* New York: United Nations, 1977.

McNeil, Donald G., Jr., "Congo Rivals Sign Cease-Fire Without 2 Rebel Groups," *New York Times*, July 11, 1999.

Miller, Judith, "Holy Warriors: Killing for the Glory of God, in a Land Far from Home," *New York Times*, January 16, 2000.

Morris, Benny, *Israel's Border Wars, 1949–1956: Arab Infiltration, Israeli Retaliation, and the Countdown to the Suez War*, New York: Oxford University Press, 1997.

Nonviolence International Southeast Asia Office, Cambodian Disarmament Survey, May–June 1998, accessed via http://www.igc.org/nonviolence/niseasia.

O'Callaghan, Sean, speech at the Center for Strategic and International Studies, Washington, D.C., September 26, 2000.

Odera, Josephine, "Small Arms and Light Weapons Proliferation: Africa: The Great Lakes Region," in *Small Arms: Big Impact*, Geneva: World Council of Churches, 1998.

Odom, William, *On Internal War: American and Soviet Approaches to Third World Clients and Insurgents*, Durham, N.C.: Duke University Press, 1992.

Pinnawala, Sisira, "Lankan Ethnic Conflict on the Internet, *Daily News*, Sri Lanka, June 25, 1998.

Quinlivan, James T., "Force Requirements in Stability Operations," *Parameters*, Vol. 24, No. 4, Winter 1995–1996.

Radu, Michael, "The Rise and Fall of the PKK," *Orbis*, Vol. 45, No. 1, Winter 2001.

Radu, Michael, and Vladimir Tismaneanu, *Latin American Revolutionaries: Groups, Goals, Methods*, Washington D.C.: Pergamon-Brassey's International Defense Publishers, Inc., 1990.

Raina, Asoka, *Inside RAW: The Story of India's Secret Service*, New Delhi: Vikas, 1981.

Rana, Swadesh, *Small Arms and Intra-State Conflicts*, UNIDIR Research Paper No. 34, United Nations Institute for Disarmament Research, 1995.

Ranetunge, Dushy, "British Charities Fund Tamil Tiger Terrors," information paper published by the Society for Peace, Unity and Human Rights (SPUR), September 2000.

_____, "LTTE Funding and Propaganda in the West," *The Island* [Sri Lanka], n.d., accessed at http://www.island.lk.

Ranstorp, Magnus, *Hizb'allah in Lebanon: The Politics of the Western Hostage Crisis*, New York: St. Martin's Press, 1997.

Rashid, Ahmed, "The Taliban: Exporting Extremism," *Foreign Affairs*, Vol. 78, No. 6, 1999.

Reno, William, "The Business of War in Liberia," *Current History*, May 1996.

_____, "Privatizing War in Sierra Leone," *Current History*, May 1997, p. 228.

_____, *Warlord Politics and African States*, Boulder, Colo.: Lynne Rienner Publishers, 1999.

Rice, Edward E., *Wars of the Third Kind: Conflict in Underdeveloped Countries*, Berkeley, Calif.: University of California Press, 1988.

Riley, S. P., "Liberia and Sierra Leone: Anarchy or Peace in West Africa?" *Conflict Studies*, Vol. 287, 1996.

Roy, Olivier, *The Failure of Political Islam*, Cambridge, Mass.: Harvard University Press, 1994.

Rubin, Barnett, "Afghanistan Under the Taliban," *Current History*, February 1999.

Saikal, Amin, "Afghanistan's Ethnic Conflict," *Survival*, Vol. 40, No. 2, 1998.

Samaranayake, Gamini, "Political Violence in Sri Lanka: A Diagnostic Approach," *Terrorism and Political Violence*, Vol. 9, No. 2, 1997.

Santina, Peter, "The People's War? The Resurgence of Maoism in Nepal," *Harvard International Review*, Vol. 23, No. 1, Spring 2001.

Schofield, Victoria, *Kashmir in Conflict: India, Pakistan and the Unfinished War*, New York: I.B. Tauris, 2000.

Sengupta, Somini, "Canada's Tamils Work for a Homeland from Afar," *New York Times,* July 16, 2000.

Shafer, D. Michael, *Deadly Paradigms: The Failure of U.S. Counterinsurgency Policy,* Princeton, N.J.: Princeton University Press, 1988.

Shain, Yossi, and Martin Sherman, "Dynamics of Disintegration: Diaspora Secession and the Paradox of Nation-States," *Nations and Nationalism,* Vol. 4, No. 3, 1998.

Sheffer, Gabriel, "Ethno-National Diasporas and Security," *Survival,* Vol. 36, No. 1, Spring 1994.

Smith, Anthony D., "Zionism and Diaspora Nationalism," *Israel Affairs,* Vol. 2, No. 2, Winter 1995.

Smith, Chris, "The Diffusion of Small Arms and Light Weapons in Pakistan and North India," *London Defence Studies Paper 20,* 1993.

_____, "The Impact of Light Weapons on Security. A Case Study of South Asia," *SIPRI Yearbook 1995,* London: Oxford University Press, 1995.

Smith, Chris, and Alex Vines, "Light Weapons Proliferation in Southern Africa," *London Defence Studies Paper 42,* 1997.

Stern, Jessica, "Pakistan's Jihad Culture," *Foreign Affairs,* Vol. 79, No. 6, November/December 2000.

Tanham, George K., and Dennis J. Duncanson, "Some Dilemmas of Counterinsurgency," *Foreign Affairs,* Vol. 48, January 1970.

Terrorist Group Celebrates Martyrs Day in Australia, internal document supplied to author by the Sri Lankan High Commission, Canberra, December 2000.

U.S. Agency for International Development, *Liberia—Complex Emergency Situation Report 1,* August 14, 1997.

Urban, Mark L., *War in Afghanistan,* New York: St. Martin's Press, 1990.

Uvin, Peter, "Ethnicity and Power in Burundi and Rwanda: Different Paths to Mass Violence," *Comparative Politics,* Vol. 31, No. 3, April 1999.

Vick, Karl, "Waging of Congo's Wars, Ore Plays a Critical Role." *International Herald Tribune,* March 20, 2001.

Volman, Daniel, "Arming Liberia's Factional Gangs," *African Policy Report,* Vol. 5, No. 15, 1996.

Weiner, Myron, "Bad Neighborhoods, Bad Neighbors: An Inquiry into the Causes of Refugee Flows," *International Security,* Vol. 21, No. 1, Summer 1996.

Weiner, Myron, ed., *International Migration and Security,* Boulder, Colo.: Westview Press, 1993.

Winchester, Mike, "Ship of Fools: Tamil Tiger's Heist of the Century," *Soldier of Fortune,* Vol. 23, No. 8, August 1998.

PERIODICALS

Africa News Service

"Crime, Treachery and West Africa's Destabilization," June 14, 2000.

Agence Presse France

"Rebels Divided on Eve of New Ceasefire in DR Congo," April 13, 2000.

The Australian

"Colombo Railway Bomb Kills at Least 40," July 25, 1996.

"Tamil Attacks," November 16, 1997.

"Malaysia Denies Thai 'Terrorist' Claims," January 5, 1998.

The Bangkok Post (Thailand)

"Khmer Arms Sold to Burma, Sri Lanka Rebels," December 6, 1995.

"Foreign 'Terrorist' Groups Designated," November 10, 1997.

"Policy No Barrier to Gun-Runners," May 28, 2000a.

"PM 'Issues Gag Order' On Rebel Activity," May 29, 2000b.

"Tamil Tigers Shopping for Arms in Cambodia," n.d.

CNN Interactive Worldwide News

"Tamils Advance; Sri Lanka Reportedly Seeks Indian Help," May 3, 2000a.

"Residents Urged to Evacuate Jaffna," May 12, 2000b.

"Tamil Tigers Urge Jaffna's Surrender, Threaten 'Bloodbath,'" May 25, 2000c.

The Courier Mail (Australia)

"Colombo Fears Suicide Bombers," November 7, 1996.

"Tamils Take Carnage to the Heart of Colombo," November 16, 1997.

Daily Mirror (Sri Lanka)

"Human Smuggling Racket Busted," June 26, 2000.

Daily News (Sri Lanka)

"Tamil Expatriates Finance LTTE Terror," June 8, 1998.

"Latest US State Department Report Reveals Details of Worldwide LTTE Extortion Racket," May 4, 1999.

"CID Bust Another Multi Billion Rupee Human Smuggling LTTE Operation," May 17, 2000.

The Deccan Herald (India)

"LTTE Warns Britain Against Ban," December 10, 2000.

The Economist

"The Covert Arms Trade," April 12, 1994.

"In Congo, War Gets Serious," September 23, 1999.

"The Diamond King," January 29, 2000a.

"The Worst Defeat," April 29, 2000b.

"Sri Lanka's Dunkirk," May 6, 2000c.

"The Militants Take Aim," August 26, 2000d.

"Going East," September 16, 2000e.

"Islamic Nerves," November 14, 2000f.

"London Calling," November 25, 2000g.

"Hitting the Tigers in their Pockets," March 10, 2001.

The Far Eastern Economic Review

"March of the Militants," March 9, 1995.

"Heart of Darkness," August 5, 1999.

The Globe and Mail (Canada)

"Without Codes of Conduct, War is No More Than Slaughter," January 17, 1998a.

"Alleged Tamil Guerrilla Arrested," September 17, 1998b.

Gulf News (United Arab Emirates)

"PKK Sold Stingers Top LTTE," October 8, 1997.

The Hindu (India)

"Pretoria Ponders Colombo's 'Concerns,'" October 30, 1998a.

"Mandela Govt. Announces Probe into LTTE Activities," November 6, 1998b.

"Kadrigamar Warns South Africa Against LTTE," November 23, 1998c.

The Hindustan Times (India)

"Canada Declares LTTE a Terrorist Organization," December 7, 1998.

India Today

"Armed to the Teeth," January 11, 1996.

Inter Press Service

"Sierra Leone: No End In Sight to Rebel Destabilization," September 23, 1992a.

"Sierra Leone: Civil War or Invasion, Peace Calls Mount," November 23, 1992b.

"Sierra Leone: Politics: Crippling Bush War Enters Its Fourth Year," March 24, 1994a.

"Sierra Leone-Liberia: Gunmen Fall From Grace," July 27, 1994b.

"Sierra Leone/Liberia: Once Hell, Now Haven," April 12, 1996.

International Herald Tribune

"Manila Dubious on Muslim Rebels," April 19, 1995.

"A Tamil Tiger Primer on International Arms Bazaar," March 10, 1998.

IISS Strategic Comments

"Tackling the Problem of Light Weapons: The 'Micro-Disarmament' Policy Debate," Vol. 4, No. 2, February 1998.

"Peace in the Congo," Vol. 5, No. 7, September 1999.

"Nepal's Maoist Insurgency: A Monarchy Under Threat," Vol. 6, No. 8, October 2000.

The Island (Sri Lanka)

"To Catch a Tiger," May 25, 1998.

"LTTE Establishes Global TV Sweep with Merger," September 20, 2000.

Jane's Sentinel Pointer

"LTTE Purchases, a Link with Cambodia," December 1996.

Jane's World Insurgency and Terrorism

"The Revolutionary United Front," May 19, 2000.

Lanka Outlook

"The LTTE Rides High in Norway," Summer 1998a.

"Tigers Go House-Hunting," December 28, 1998b.

The National Post (Canada)

"Tamil Fundraiser Loses Final Appeal of His Deportation," June 17, 1999.

"Underground to Canada," March 25, 2000a.

"He Says He's Sri Lanka's 'Oscar Schindler,'" March 27, 2000b.

"Money Trail: Financing War from Canada," June 3, 2000c.

"Sri Lanka's Civil War," June 3, 2000d.

"CSIS Warned Ottawa of Terror Fronts," December 9, 2000e.

New York Times

"Congo Rebels' Debts to Foreign Backers Remain Unclear," May 22, 1997.

"Rebels and Soldiers Reported Killed in Central Asia Region," August 14, 2000.

New York Times on the Web

"Africa's Diamond Wars," June 4, 2000.

Periscope Daily Defense Capsules

"Sierra Leone: Rebels Said to Join Liberia War," May 4, 1993.

Periscope Daily News

"Sierra Leone: Liberian Say Rebels Store Arms," February 2, 1994.

The Perspective

"Diamonds, War and State Collapse in Liberia and Sierra Leone," July 18, 2000.

SBS Dateline (Australia)

"Behind the Tamil Tigers," October 4, 2000.

The Scotsman

"Diamonds with Ultimate Price Tag," July 1, 2000.

The Sunday Telegraph (UK)

"Liberia Chief Fuels 'Diamond War': The President is Flying Out Gems on Libyan Jets to Fund the Conflict in Sierra Leone," May 28, 2000.

The Sunday Times (South Africa)

"Guns Threaten Our Hard Won Freedom," April 30, 1995.

The Sunday Times (Sri Lanka)

"Tigers Eye SA for Base," October 25, 1998.

"Tiger Arms Ship in High Sea Drama," May 9, 1999.

Times of India

"LTTE Links with Human Smuggling Racket Exposed," March 20, 2000.

Washington Post

"State Department Listing of Terror Groups Upheld," June 26, 1999.

"Congo Looks for Leadership," October 30, 2000a.

"For Refugees, Hazardous Haven in Guinea," November 6, 2000b.

Zimbabwe Independent

"Diamond Company to Pay Zimbabwe for Role in Congo," June 9, 2000.